Introduction

'Look, Gabriel!' cried Miss Rachel, flashing the jewel in the sunlight. It was as large as a bird's egg, the colour of the harvest moon, a deep yellow that sucked your eyes into it so you saw nothing else.

Wealthy young Englishwoman, Rachel Verinder, is fascinated by the huge yellow diamond that she is given for her eighteenth birthday. But it soon becomes clear that the jewel brings disaster with it. Known as the Moonstone, long ago a terrible curse was put on anyone who stole it, and it was guarded by three Hindu priests. Then in 1794, Rachel's uncle, Colonel John Herncastle, stole the jewel. Rejected by his family, he dies a tragic, lonely death. But in his will he gives the diamond to his niece as a birthday present. The jewel is stolen during the night that follows Rachel's birthday party. Could the curse have begun again?

The immediate suspects are three Indians who recently visited the house, since they are believed to be Hindu priests who have come to get the Moonstone back. But it seems that they could not have stolen the diamond and that the thief must be someone who slept in the house on the night of the theft. A famous detective, Sergeant Cuff, is called in to investigate, and it soon becomes clear that Rachel, who has locked herself in her room, knows something about the jewel's disappearance. However, she refuses to say what she knows. Can Sergeant Cuff solve the mystery?

The Moonstone, by Wilkie Collins, was first published in parts in the magazine *All the Year Round* in 1868, and it appeared as a complete novel later the same year. It was hugely successful.

But Collins' importance in English literature comes not only from the quality of his work but also from its originality. *The Moonstone* contained the first example of a professional detective who is called in to solve a crime. The great twentieth-century poet T. S. Eliot described *The Moonstone* as 'the first, the longest and the best of modern English detective novels.'

The plot is complicated and the question of who stole the Moonstone seems impossible to solve. The guests who slept at the house on the night of the theft include Franklin Blake, Rachel's attractive, likeable cousin, who has known Rachel since childhood and is in love with her, and another relative, Godfrey Ablewhite, a good-looking lawyer who is also in love with Rachel. The servants are also suspects. Gabriel Betteredge, the trusted Head Servant of Lady Verinder (Rachel's mother), is above suspicion. But what about Rosanna Spearman, a maid who used to be a thief? The reader will be fascinated as the mystery becomes more and more puzzling until the dramatic conclusion when the thief is at last revealed.

Wilkie (William) Collins, the son of a landscape painter, was born in London in 1824. He was educated privately but considered that his real education was acquired during trips around Europe with his family. He discovered his gift for storytelling while he was still a schoolboy. As a young adult, he worked for a tea importer for a few years and then studied law. He also considered being an artist. However, he soon realized that his real love was writing. He wrote a book about his father, which was published in 1848, and a historical novel called *Antonina or the Fall of Rome* (1850).

Collins traveled a lot, spending time in France, Italy and the United States, often with his friend, the great writer Charles Dickens, whom he met in 1851, and who had a great influence on him. He worked with Dickens on theatrical and writing projects and wrote many articles and short stories for his magazines. The two remained good friends until Dickens's death.

Collins wrote articles, short stories and plays, but his real talent was for writing novels. He wrote several during the 1850s, the best of which was *Basil* (1852), an exciting mystery story. However, it was in the 1860s that Collins wrote his most famous mystery novels. These novels made him one of the most popular writers of the time and they remain popular today. These were *The Woman in White* (1860) and *The Moonstone* (1868). Other novels of this period include *No Name* (1862) and *Armadale* (1866).

The novels that Collins wrote after 1870 were less successful, although his books still sold well. He was repeatedly ill during this period, and he also seemed to be more concerned with social issues, such as divorce, than with the quality of his stories.

His private life was very unusual for those times of strict social morality; he lived for years with a woman called Caroline Graves, and at the same time kept Martha Rudd, the mother of his three children, in a second home. He did not marry either of these women. He died in 1889.

Collins is known today for his two greatest novels, *The Woman in White* (also available as a Penguin Reader) and *The Moonstone*. Although T. S. Eliot described *The Moonstone* as the first full-length detective story, the statement is perhaps truer of *The Woman in White*, since the hero and heroine, although not professional detectives, act as detectives as they try to discover the story's central mystery.

Collins's novels have sold widely in Britain, the United States and Europe, and have been translated into many other languages. Collins's advice to other writers is still widely followed: 'Make 'em laugh, make 'em cry, make 'em wait.'

During the period that *The Moonstone* was written, the territories that the British ruled abroad, known as 'the British Empire', were steadily increasing, and India was the Empire's most precious possession. Britain's domination of India began in 1600, when a trading organization called the East India Company steadily gained possession of Indian territories, until by the mid-nineteenth century a large part of India was owned by the British. In 1858, the British Queen Victoria became the formal ruler of British India. Writers such as Wilkie Collins were interested in Indian culture, and this interest is reflected in *The Moonstone*, with the diamond and its curse, and the three Hindu priests. The Hindu priests who have come to England to recover the Moonstone, though willing to kill in order to obtain the diamond, are shown to be educated and clever.

The Moonstone takes place against a background of upper-class wealth, and Lady Verinder, her family and relatives are all rich. But Collins was interested in social issues, and the two servants who play an important part in the novel are sympathetically treated. Betteredge, Lady Verinder's Head Servant, who is the story-teller in one part of the novel, is clearly an intelligent man, and he is kind to the unhappy maid, Rosanna Spearman, one of the chief suspects.

The drug opium, which by the nineteenth century was imported from India to the West in huge quantities, plays a part in this story. Opium was used as a means of controlling pain, and one of the characters in the novel, Gabriel Jennings, a medical assistant, uses it during the last stages of his own fatal illness. Collins was very aware of opium's effects, as he had a painful illness and used opium to lessen the pain. He used the drug so much, in fact, during the writing of *The Moonstone* that he later said that he had no memory of writing large parts of the novel.

The Moonstone

WILKIE COLLINS

Level 6

Retold by David Wharry
Series Editors: Andy Hopkins and Jocelyn Potter

Pearson Education Limited
Edinburgh Gate, Harlow,
Essex CM20 2JE, England
and Associated Companies throughout the world.

ISBN: 978-1-4058-8268-2

The Moonstone was first published in 1868
This adaptation first published by Penguin Books 1994
Published by Addison Wesley Longinan Ltd and Penguin Books Ltd 1998
New edition first published 1999
This edition first published 2008

1 3 5 7 9 10 8 6 4 2

Text copyright © David Whitry 1994
Illustrations copyright © Victor G. Ambrus 1994
All rights reserved

The moral right of the adapter and of the illustrator has been asserted

Typeset by Graphicraft Ltd, Hong Kong
Set in 11/14pt Bembo
Printed in China
SWTC/01

Published by Pearson Education Ltd in association with
Penguin Books Ltd, both companies being subsidiaries of Pearson Plc

For a complete list of the titles available in the Penguin Readers series please write to your local
Pearson Longman office or to: Penguin Readers Marketing Department, Pearson Education,
Edinburgh Gate, Harlow, Essex CM20 2JE, England.

Contents

The Moonstone started certain traditions in detective novels that still continue today. The situation where a crime is committed in an enclosed space (for example, a house or train) with a limited number of suspects, is still used very successfully today in detective stories. Similarly, Collins started the tradition of the brilliant professional detective. Sergeant Cuff is described as 'a miserable-looking figure in black' who loves roses and whose eyes are 'as sharp as knives'. His skills as a famous detective are far above those of the local police detective, Superintendent Seegrave, who is sent to solve the case and who is quickly dismissed. Since then, many other writers have written detective stories that involve a detective with extraordinary investigative powers. The most famous example is Sherlock Holmes, the detective invented by English writer Arthur Conan Doyle at the end of the nineteenth century.

In both *The Moonstone* and *The Woman in White*, Collins also experimented with a new way of telling a story: the stories are told from the point of view of a number of different characters. In *The Moonstone*, the characters of two of the story-tellers come through particularly clearly. We soon understand that Gabriel Betteredge, whose narrative begins the novel, is kind and reliable. In contrast, Miss Clack, who tells the second part of the story, is amusingly dislikable, claiming to be religious when she is obviously an unpleasant person.

The Moonstone is generally agreed to be among the great nineteenth century English novels. At least five films have been made of it, the first in 1915. Detective stories are jokingly known as 'whodunits' (in other words, 'Who did it?'), and *The Moonstone* has a good claim to be one of the best whodunits ever written.

Taken From an Old Family Letter

I am writing to my family to explain why I am no longer my cousin's friend, and to end the misunderstanding my silence has caused.

My disagreement with my cousin, John Herncastle, began in India in 1791, during the capture of the town of Seringapatam under General Baird. Before the battle the camp was alive with talk of gold and jewels in the Palace of Seringapatam, and particularly of a huge yellow diamond. Ancient Indian writings describe the diamond, known as the Moonstone, whose place was originally in the forehead of the Hindu God of the Moon.

In the eleventh century a golden temple was built for the Moon-God in the holy city of Benares. The god Vishnu appeared in a dream to the three priests who guarded the diamond. He ordered that it should continue to be guarded by three priests, night and day until the end of time. Vishnu foresaw disaster for anyone who might take the holy stone, disaster for his family and for all those who received it after him.

For centuries, three priests kept watch over the Moonstone until, in the early eighteenth century, the temple was destroyed by a Muslim army. Their leader, Aurungzebe, broke up the Moon-God and took the jewel. Powerless to get back their holy treasure by force, the priests followed the Muslim army, watching and waiting.

Many years went by, Aurungzebe died a terrible death, and the Moonstone passed (carrying disaster with it) from one unlucky hand to another, always accompanied by three priests, waiting for their chance. In 1794, the Sultan of Seringapatam fitted the jewel into the handle of one of his ceremonial knives. Unknown to him, three Hindus, disguised as servants, were keeping watch in his palace.

The night before the attack I and other officers laughed at my cousin when he became angry with us for not taking the story seriously.

1

'The Moonstone will have its revenge on you and your family!'
cried the Indian before dying.

We entered the palace at dusk the next day. The day's fighting had whipped my cousin into an excitement close to madness. I was sent to stop soldiers stealing gold and jewels. While I was trying to control the men I heard terrible screams. Rushing through a door I saw two Indians lying dead and a third, badly wounded, falling beside Herncastle who held a long knife, dripping with blood. A large precious stone in the handle flashed as he turned to me. 'The Moonstone will have its revenge on you and your family!' cried the Indian before dying. Herncastle turned to me, laughing like a madman, staring at the jewel. Soldiers came in. 'Clear the room!' he shouted. I did so and left immediately, horrified by what I had seen.

PART 1   THE LOSS OF THE DIAMOND

The events told by Gabriel Betteredge,
Head Servant of Lady Julia Verinder

Chapter 1   A Record of the Facts

This morning (May 21st 1850), my lady's nephew, Mr Franklin Blake, said to me: 'Betteredge, I've seen Mr Bruff, our lawyer, and we talked about the loss of the diamond two years ago. He thinks a complete record of the facts ought to be put down in writing. And I agree with him. The story should be told and I believe we've found a way to do it. Everyone will tell their part of the story in turn, beginning at the beginning. I have a letter telling how my uncle got hold of the diamond in India. Next we must tell how the stone reached my aunt's house in Yorkshire two years ago; and then, of course, how it was lost twelve hours after it was given to Rachel. Nobody knows more than you, dear Betteredge, about what went on in the house during that time. So your narrative must be the first.'

I have a clear memory for a man of over seventy. However, I did what you probably would have done: I modestly declared that I was incapable of such a task. But young Mr Franklin insisted, and here I am at my desk two hours later, realizing I may have bitten off more than I can chew. Oh, well, here goes . . .

♦

I worked for Lord Herncastle, and after he died, when Miss Julia, his youngest daughter, married Sir John Verinder, I came with her to Sir John's house here in Yorkshire. I married a local girl, but five years later she died, poor soul, leaving me with my little girl, Penelope. Soon afterwards,

4

Sir John died and my lady was left with her only child, Miss Rachel. My lady made sure that Penelope was educated, and when she was old enough she became Miss Rachel's maid.

My lady promoted me. I became manager of her farms in Yorkshire and carried on this work until, on Christmas Day 1847, my lady invited me to tea. 'Gabriel,' she said, 'It is time to work less. From today you will give up the outdoor work and simply look after the servants here in the house.' I protested, but looking out over the cold grey hills I knew she was right.

Chapter 2   Three Indian Men

I shall begin with the morning of 24th May 1848. My lady called me into her sitting-room. 'My nephew, Franklin Blake, has returned from abroad,' she said. 'He is coming to stay until Rachel's birthday next month. He will arrive tomorrow.' I calculated he was twenty-five years old. I hadn't seen him since he was a boy – the nicest little boy I've ever known. The fun he and Rachel had playing together! He'd gone abroad, to schools in Germany, Italy and France, and had then wandered around Europe, no doubt borrowing everywhere he went (I remembered he still owed me a halfpenny). He spent money like water – probably on those continental women he mentioned to me in a letter once. His yearly allowance of seven hundred pounds disappeared in an instant!

Next morning, my lady and Miss Rachel, expecting Mr Franklin at dinner time, drove out to lunch with friends. I inspected our guest's bedroom, left a bottle of wine to warm in the soft summer air, and was about to sit down outside in my favourite chair when I heard a sound like a drum. I went round to the front of the house. Three dark-skinned Indian men in white coats, each with a drum, were looking at the house. Behind them stood a small English boy. One of them, a man of most elegant manners, told me in excellent English that they were travelling magicians. He asked permission to perform tricks to my lady. I said she was out and ordered them to leave. The man bowed beautifully and they left. I returned to my chair until Penelope woke me, excited, saying the Indians were planning to do some kind of harm to Mr Franklin. She was in the garden when they left. On the road, thinking they were unseen, one of them had poured ink into the boy's hand and made signs over his head. 'Can you see the Englishman from abroad?' the Indian asked him. 'I see him,' said the boy, staring at the ink. 'Has he got *It* with him?' asked the man. 'Yes,' answered the boy. 'Will he come here tonight as he said?' asked another. 'I can't see any more,' said the boy, 'My mind is full of fog.' They made more signs over the boy, woke him up, and walked off towards town.

Penelope was sick with worry. 'Father, what does *It* mean?'

'We'll ask Mr Franklin when he comes,' I replied.

Chapter 3   The Will

I was nearly asleep again when Nancy, the kitchen maid, rushed out, bumping into my chair. 'I'm sorry sir,' she said, 'But Rosanna's late for dinner again. She fainted again this morning, and asked to go out for some air. She'll be at the Shivering Sand, no doubt.' I had a kind of pity for Rosanna so I decided to fetch her myself.

Four months before, in London, my lady had visited a home for women who had just been released from prison. She met

Rosanna Spearman, who had been a thief, an extremely plain-looking girl with a deformed shoulder. The Director recommended her, saying she deserved a second chance. A week later, she began as our second housemaid.

Only my lady, Miss Rachel and I knew about her past, and Rosanna was grateful for our trust in her. She was hard-working and polite, but the servants didn't like her silent, lonely ways. They thought she thought she was superior to them.

Our house is near the sea, with beautiful walks in all directions. But a quarter of a mile away is an ugly, lonely little bay that has the most horrible quicksands. When the tide turns, something happens down under the surface. The whole face of the quicksand begins to tremble. No boat ever comes into that bay – even the birds seem to avoid it. Yet it was Rosanna's favourite place.

When I arrived, I saw her sitting in the grey coat she wore to hide her shoulder, looking out to sea. She was crying. I gave her my handkerchief, sat down beside her, and asked her what was wrong. 'It's my past, sir,' she said, drying her eyes. 'You must forget all that,' I said. She took my hand and squeezed it. 'Why do you like this miserable place?' I asked. 'A strange kind of magic seems to pull me here,' she replied. 'Sometimes I think my grave is waiting for me here.' She put her hand on my shoulder. 'Dear Mr Betteredge, I'm trying to deserve your trust, but some-times I feel there's no future for me here.' She pointed at the quicksand. 'Look!' she said. The tide was turning. The whole face of the sands was beginning to tremble. 'Isn't it wonderful? Isn't it terrible?' she cried. 'Throw a stone in, sir. Watch the sand suck it down!'

I heard a voice shout, 'Betteredge!' Rosanna jumped up and looked towards the woods behind us. I was astonished by the sudden change in her. Her cheeks turned a beautiful red, her whole being seemed to brighten with a kind of breathless surprise. I looked round and saw a handsome, beautifully dressed young gentleman coming out of the trees. His smile would have made even the quicksand smile. He sat down beside me, put his arm around me and said, 'Dear old Betteredge, I owe you a halfpenny.' He looked up at Rosanna, their eyes met and her cheeks went an even deeper red. Seemingly confused, she turned and left us suddenly. It was very unlike her. 'She's an odd one,' said Mr Franklin. 'Why on earth did she do that?' I couldn't – then – offer any explanation for her behaviour.

'Welcome back, Mr Franklin,' I said. He had changed, but he still had the same bright, straightforward look in his eyes. 'I've a reason for coming earlier than expected,' he said. 'I've been followed by a dark-skinned man in London for the last few days. I took an early train to lose him. Tell me about those Indians who came today.'

'How on earth do you know about them?' I asked.

'I saw Penelope. "My father will tell you all about the magicians," she said. She's pretty, Betteredge, and she says your edge is better than ever!' His gay mood died away when I told him. Looking worried, he took a small packet from his pocket. *It means this*,' he said. 'My wicked uncle's famous diamond. He left it to Rachel in his will. My father, who is managing his brother's affairs, gave it to me to bring here. The will states that it must be given to her on her birthday.'

'Your father is managing his affairs!' I said. 'He hated him! So did my lady. She forbade him to ever enter her house again.'

Let me explain. It became public knowledge that Colonel Herncastle had got possession of the Moonstone in dishonest circumstances. When he returned from India, he was avoided by everyone. For years he led a lonely life, never showing the diamond to anyone. It was said that he was afraid it would cost him his life. Almost two years ago, he came to my lady's house in London, on the night of Miss Rachel's birthday. I was told a gentleman wanted to see me. I left the party upstairs and met him in the hall. He was old, wasted, but looked as wild and wicked as ever. 'Tell my sister,' he said, 'that I have come to wish my niece a happy birthday.' I went upstairs with the message. Controlling her anger, my lady said coldly, 'Tell Colonel Herncastle that Rachel is busy, and that I do not wish to see him.' When I told the Colonel downstairs his grey eyes settled on me and he laughed softly. 'Thank you, Betteredge,' he said. 'Never mind. I shall remember my niece's birthday in the future.' He left without another word, and the next I heard of him was that he had died, six months ago.

Mr Franklin tapped the packet. 'I have made some interesting discoveries at Mr Bruff's office,' he said. 'An old family letter says that *It* was the object of an ancient holy curse, and also the object of a promise by three Hindu priests. If the Colonel knew this – and he almost certainly did – was he deliberately trying to pass on the curse to the sister he hated, by giving *It* to her innocent daughter?'

I couldn't understand my own alarm. Who, in this age of progress, could believe that the peace of our English country house could be suddenly ruined by an Indian diamond with a Hindu curse on it?

Mr Franklin read my thoughts. 'I noticed the man following me after I took the stone out of the bank.' He looked around him suspiciously. 'You must understand that the idea of chosen servants of an old Hindu superstition waiting for years for the opportunity to get back their holy stone is perfectly normal – in the Oriental way of thinking, that is. Their religion has given them a different idea of patience to ours. The Colonel knew this, and made clever arrangements to hide the stone during his lifetime.' He lay down. 'I don't want to alarm my aunt unnecessarily,' he said, staring up at the sky. 'Yet I feel she must be warned. If you were in my place, Betteredge, what would you do?'

'Sir,' I said, 'Today is May 25th. The Colonel's will states that Miss Rachel must be given the diamond on her birthday, June 21st. We have over three weeks to wait and see what happens. Time will tell us what to do. Until then, put the stone in the bank in Fritzinghall (our nearest town). Do it now, before the ladies return.'

He jumped up and pulled me to my feet. 'Betteredge,' he said, 'you're worth your weight in gold.' We returned to the house and he left for Fritzinghall. I wondered whether I wasn't dreaming, the morning's events had put me in such a spin.

Chapter 4   A Shadow

When my lady and Miss Rachel returned in the afternoon, I told them that Mr Franklin had arrived, but had had to go into Fritzinghall on business. Shortly afterwards, Penelope told me she thought Rosanna had fallen hopelessly in love with Mr Franklin. She was behaving strangely, happy one minute, sad the next, and she kept asking questions about him. She had written his name in her sewing box and taken a lot of trouble with her hair, crying as she looked at her deformed shoulder in the mirror. I almost laughed: a poor plain housemaid falling in love with a gentleman!

Mr Franklin returned shortly before dinner. I was relieved to hear that he hadn't met the Indians and that the Moonstone was in the bank.

Penelope said Miss Rachel took an unusual amount of trouble with her hair before dinner. A head servant never serves dinner – unfortunately, as I was curious to know how they got on together after all these years. Later, we heard them singing happily together with my lady at the piano. Later still, I took whisky to Mr Franklin in the smoking-room. 'She's the most charming girl I've seen since I came back to England,' he said.

Towards midnight, when Samuel (my second-in-command) and I had locked up the house, I went out to get some air. The moon was full and the air was still. I could hear the sea rolling in over the Shivering Sand. Then I heard a sound, much closer, and saw a shadow disappear round the corner of the house. I heard feet running away. But by the time I reached the corner, whoever it was had disappeared. Samuel and I took guns, searched the garden but found nothing. Returning, I saw something shining on the ground. It was a small bottle of black ink.

Chapter 5   Rivals

The next day I showed the bottle to Mr Franklin. 'They believe the boy can see where eyes cannot see,' he said. He smiled. 'If he can see into the bank, they won't trouble us *here* any longer.' Maybe the boy could see through walls because they never came near the house again in the weeks before Rachel's birthday. They simply remained in Fritzinghall, doing their magician's trade.

On May 29th, Miss Rachel and Mr Franklin decided to make a horrible smell and a great mess and spoil a door. Mr Franklin was an expert on 'decorative painting', and had invented a special way of mixing paint. Special substances were sent from London, the revolutionary paint was mixed, and smelled so bad that it made even the dogs sneeze. The unlucky door was Miss Rachel's sitting-room door. For days they were as busy as bees, spoiling it with complicated designs, and the pleasure they took in each other's company became obvious to everyone. There was no doubt that Mr Franklin was in love. Miss Rachel's feelings, however, were not so obvious. Some (such as Penelope) were sure they would marry. I doubted it.

Miss Rachel is the finest, most graceful of women. Dark, beautifully shaped, she is a pleasure to the eyes. Although cheeky, playful and secretive by nature, there is nothing false about her (I have never known her lie or break her word). She has however, one fault. Many times I have heard my lady say 'Rachel's worst enemy is herself!' Yes, I know few as devilishly stubborn as her. She only ever goes one way – her own. Which brings me to my opinion of her views about marriage.

My lady's sister married Mr Ablewhite, a banker, and they live near Fritzinghall. On June 12th, an invitation to the birthday party was sent to their son, Mr Godfrey Ablewhite, in London – the man I believed she loved. Mr Godfrey, a lawyer, was taller and finer looking than Mr Franklin, and most popular with the ladies, being well known for his tireless work as president of several women's charities. The poor and homeless women of England depended on him! And what a public speaker! I heard him perform once at a charity meeting. Who could not give money to a man like this?

Mr Godfrey accepted the invitation. No doubt sensing the competition, Mr Franklin tried everything to win Miss Rachel's hand. He even gave up smoking – she hated the smell of his cigars. Without their calming effect, he began to sleep badly. Penelope believed this sacrifice had impressed Miss Rachel. Perhaps, but in her bedroom she had a photograph of Mr Godfrey speaking at a charity meeting.

On June 16th Mr Franklin's chances got even worse (to my mind) when a French lawyer visited the house. He had a heated conversation with Mr Franklin and my lady. Apparently, Miss

Rachel said some severe things to Mr Franklin that evening, about people he knew on the Continent, about a woman, and about a debt – that my lady had paid for him. The next day, however, they seemed to be friends again, singing and joking as they decorated the door. Penelope said Mr Franklin had made an offer – which had been neither accepted nor refused.

On the 19th, Dr Candy came to see Rosanna. The poor girl had lost her appetite, often showed signs of crying, was behaving most strangely, and was always putting herself in Mr Franklin's way (he never even noticed her, of course). My lady noticed the change. Trying to protect her, I said she had problems with her health. Dr Candy said it was her nerves. My lady suggested a change of air, work on one of our farms. Rosanna begged to be allowed to stay.

On the 20th, a note from Mr Godfrey came from Fritzinghall, saying he would come over the following afternoon. With it came a beautifully decorated Chinese box for Miss Rachel. Mr Franklin had given her a plain piece of jewellery worth only half as much.

Chapter 6   The Moonstone

June 21st, Rachel's birthday, was cloudy at dawn, but the sky soon cleared. After breakfast, Mr Franklin and I met to discuss the Moonstone. He was nervous and rather absent-minded, either because he was thinking about Miss Rachel or perhaps because of his sleeplessness (he was still determined not to smoke). We agreed that since nothing had happened there was no reason to alarm my lady, and that he should remove the stone from the bank after lunch and return, if possible, with Mr Godfrey. Afterwards, he and Miss Rachel went back to decorating the door. All morning Penelope mixed the paints, until, at three o'clock, they proudly declared it was finished. It was not unpleasant to look at. It certainly looked better than it smelled.

Mr Franklin rode to Fritzinghall and after giving directions for the dinner, I sat down in my chair. I woke when he returned with Mr Godfrey. The fine young lawyer greeted everyone most politely but, strangely, like Mr Franklin, there was a sort of cloud over him.

I had a quick word with Mr Franklin in the hall. 'Have you got the diamond, sir?' He nodded. 'Did you see any Indians?' He shook his head and went into the living-room to see Miss Rachel. About half an hour later, I heard screams coming from the room.

I knocked, went in, and saw Miss Rachel staring, fascinated, at the diamond in her hand. 'Extraordinary, extraordinary!' exclaimed Mr Godfrey, clapping his hands like an overgrown child. Mr Franklin was looking anxiously at my lady who was reading her brother's will. She turned to me, frowning. 'Come to my room in half an hour, Betteredge,' she said, and left the room. 'Look, Gabriel!' cried Miss Rachel, flashing the jewel in the sunlight. It was as large as a bird's egg, the colour of the harvest moon, a deep yellow that sucked your eyes into it so you saw nothing else. Curiously enough, as we stood admiring it, Mr Godfrey (his admiring eyes on Miss Rachel) said, 'It's only mineral, my dear, just a piece of very hard stone.'

Later, my lady told me that she had the blackest suspicions of the Colonel's motives and had decided to get the Moonstone out of Rachel's possession. I didn't tell her about the Indians.

Penelope came in as I was dressing for dinner. 'News for you, father!' she said. 'I saw Miss Rachel and that nasty scheming ladies' charity man go into the rose garden arm in arm, laughing, and come back walking apart, with very long faces. He stopped her and said, "Do you want me to stay – as if nothing had happened?" She turned on him. "Yes," she said, "you've

It was as large as a bird's egg, the colour of the harvest moon, a deep yellow that sucked your eyes into it so you saw nothing else.

accepted my mother's invitation. Now, let's forget what happened, Godfrey, please." She left him. He stood there, saying, "Annoying ... annoying ..." Isn't it wonderful! I told you Mr Franklin's the man!' I heard wheels outside – the first guests. I reached the hall just in time to welcome Mr and Mrs Ablewhite.

Chapter 7   The Indians Return

Twenty-four guests sat down to dinner. I will mention only a few.

Miss Rachel, the queen of the evening, wore her wonderful birthday present. Cleverly, Mr Franklin had fixed it to her dress with silver wire. On her left sat Dr Candy, from Fritzinghall, a pleasant man, wise in his medicine and fond of a joke. On her right sat the explorer Mr Murthwaite, a tall quiet man with a watchful eye. He had spent years wandering about India. After a long look at the diamond, he said, 'Miss Rachel, if you ever go to India, don't take *that* with you – your life wouldn't be worth sixpence.'

As the meal went on I became sadly aware that the party lacked life. Nobody had their usual appetite, there were often gaps in the talk, and even old jokers like Dr Candy had nothing funny to say. Normally brilliant conversationalists seemed almost dull – Mr Godfrey, for instance. He spent the whole meal in serious discussion with Miss Clack, a distant cousin of Miss Rachel's. She was one of his ladies' charity friends, a most religiously-minded woman. However, I noticed she had a rather low-cut dress and a fondness for champagne.

Not even Mr Franklin was able to brighten up the evening. On the contrary! Having annoyed our local priest with his ideas on marriage, he made Dr Candy angry with his views on medicine. The argument ended on the subject of his sleepless nights. Dr Candy told him that his nerves were out of order and that medicine could cure his sleep problems. Mr Franklin replied that medicine was like a blind man in the dark. My lady wisely interrupted them, and invited the ladies to leave the gentlemen over their wine.

Shortly afterwards, as I was filling Mr Franklin's glass, I nearly jumped out of my skin. It was the sound of a drum. The Indians had returned! I ran outside, only to see my lady welcoming the three men and the boy. And beside her stood Miss Rachel, with the diamond shining on her dress! Immediately, Mr Franklin went and stood next to her, ready for anything. Mr Murthwaite spoke to them in their language, his words instantly wiping the smiles off their faces. They bowed to him in the most polite and snaky way, and their chief, his dark skin now slightly grey, turned to us and said, 'There will be no magic tonight.' Everyone except Mr Murthwaite, Mr Franklin and myself went inside. I led the Indians to the gates and they left. When I returned, Mr Murthwaite and Mr Franklin were talking. 'Gabriel,' said Mr Franklin, 'Mr Murthwaite suspects that they are priests. I've told him the story behind Rachel's present.'

'They're certainly not magicians,' said Mr Murthwaite. 'How you escaped them so far, I can't imagine. You're lucky to be alive Mr Blake. Yes, there can only be one reason for their presence here: to return the diamond to the forehead of their god.'

'Priests!' I said. 'Murdering thieves, you mean!'

'They're only acting according to their religion,' he said.

'They've seen the diamond now,' said Mr Franklin.

'Take it to Amsterdam tomorrow,' said Murthwaite. 'Have it cut into several smaller ones. It will no longer be the Moonstone, therefore no longer holy to its – to those who once owned it.'

'What about tonight?' I asked. 'They may come back.'

'No, they won't risk that,' Murthwaite replied. 'But let your hunting dogs loose in the garden just in case.' He and

Mr Franklin went inside and I sat down, sweating, wondering what to do. Penelope came out later with a report from the drawing-room. Mr Murthwaite had fallen asleep. Mr Franklin had deliberately annoyed Mr Godfrey by making fun of women's charities. Dr Candy had mysteriously disappeared, mysteriously returned and had a whispered conversation with Mr Godfrey. In about an hour they would all be leaving.

I could hear distant thunder. I went out with two of the dogs and made a final search of the garden. It was beginning to rain hard as I returned. Dr Candy was the last guest to leave. I was concerned because his carriage had no roof. He boasted that all doctors had skins like ducks and drove away in the rain laughing at his joke.

Chapter 8   The Theft

When my lady had said goodnight to Mr Franklin and Mr Godfrey, she looked hard at her brother's gift shining on her daughter's dress. 'Rachel,' she asked, 'where will you put your diamond tonight?' Rachel thought. 'In my Indian cabinet, of course – the one with all the drawers.' Her mother frowned. 'My dear, it has no lock on it.' Miss Rachel, happy, light-headed, replied, 'But mamma, there are no thieves in the house.'

'Why not let *me* keep it tonight?' said my lady. Miss Rachel refused. 'Then come to me first thing tomorrow, Rachel,' said my lady, going upstairs. Miss Rachel said goodnight next, simply shaking hands with Mr Godfrey, but giving Mr Franklin an extraordinarily tender smile. I began, at that moment, to believe that Penelope might be right after all.

'I'm going to let the dogs loose, tonight,' I told Mr Franklin as soon as she was gone. 'We'll decide on what is to be done tomorrow morning,' he said. He looked pale and tired. I advised him to take some whisky and water to help him sleep. Mr Godfrey came over to say he agreed and tried, in the friendliest way, to persuade him to drink something. Mr Franklin refused politely and the two rivals went upstairs together. A minute later Mr Franklin called down: 'Perhaps I will have that whisky.' Samuel went up with the drink, I let the dogs loose, and when we had shut up the house, I took my old bones up to bed and lay awake all night listening to the rain and the wind outside.

At 8 a.m., Penelope rushed into the kitchen. 'Father, the diamond's gone!' she screamed, and dragged me upstairs. Miss Rachel was standing as white as a sheet beside her Indian cabinet, one of its drawers open, empty. 'I saw Miss Rachel put the diamond in there last night!' Penelope cried.

'Is this true, miss?' I asked. With a look that was completely unlike her, with a voice that didn't seem to be her own, she simply answered, 'The diamond is gone!' and went into her bedroom and locked the door.

My lady came in, stone-faced, knocked at Miss Rachel's door and was let in. The two gentlemen rushed in. Mr Godfrey held up his hands in helpless disbelief. Mr Franklin, however, showed himself to be more clear-headed – perhaps because that night he had slept well for the first time since he had given up smoking. He ordered us to search the room and knocked on Miss Rachel's bedroom door. My lady came out. The door was immediately shut behind her and locked from the inside. 'The loss of the diamond has thrown Rachel into a state of shock,' she said. 'She won't speak about it, not even to me.'

'We must call the police,' said Mr Franklin. 'They must arrest the Indians immediately – if it's not already too late.' Seeing my lady's and Mr Godfrey's surprise, he added, 'All I can say now is they certainly have the diamond. I'll ride to Fritzinghall immediately.' I hurried out after him and asked how the Indians could have got into the house. 'One may have got in while the guests were leaving,' he shouted, riding off. 'But how did the thief escape? I inspected the house. All the doors and windows were locked. And how could he have possibly escaped the dogs?'

After breakfast – theft or no theft, one must have one's breakfast – I told my lady the truth about the Indian's plot. She was extremely shocked but, surprisingly, seemed more concerned about her daughter. 'I've never seen her behave so strangely,' she said. 'The loss of the jewel has had an effect on her brain.'

Mr Godfrey was behaving strangely too, wandering about in an uneasy, aimless way. He was of weaker metal than I had thought. But we were all uneasy. The servants were suspecting one another. The Moonstone had turned us all upside down.

Mr Franklin returned before eleven. 'Superintendent Seegrave is coming,' he said. 'But it's useless. The case is hopeless.'

'Why? Have the Indians escaped, sir?' I asked.

'Those Indians have been imprisoned unfairly,' he replied. 'Police enquiries proved that they returned to Fritzinghall and stayed in their hotel all night. Nevertheless, in case of any further discoveries, they're being kept in prison for a week.' But if they were innocent, I asked myself, who had taken the Moonstone?

Ten minutes later, Seegrave and his men arrived. I knew him well: a large, loud man. Mr Franklin immediately told him the investigation was hopeless. Seegrave found no signs of a forced entry. 'Someone inside must have stolen the stone,' he declared confidently. The servants, feeling suspected, followed him up to Miss Rachel's sitting-room like a cloud of angry bees. 'Look!' he said, pointing to a smear in the paint on the door. 'Someone's dress has brushed against the wet paint.' Everyone except Rosanna crowded round to see. 'Back to work, all of you!' he ordered. I noticed Rosanna leave immediately. Seegrave then searched the room, found nothing, and asked to see Penelope. 'Now, young woman,' he said sharply, 'I want the truth.'

'Are you accusing me?' my daughter replied fiercely. After I had smoothed things over, she told him how she had seen Miss Rachel put the diamond in the drawer before going to bed. Next morning, at eight o'clock, when she brought Miss Rachel her breakfast, she had found the drawer open, empty.

Seegrave knocked on Miss Rachel's bedroom door. 'Go away! I have nothing to say to anyone!' she shouted from inside. Seeing his anger and surprise, I told him Miss Rachel was ill and asked him to wait and see her later.

'Seegrave is a fool,' Mr Franklin whispered downstairs, before going out on to the terrace with Mr Godfrey. Miss Rachel came downstairs as pale as death, ignoring the Superintendent, who tried to speak to her. She went out on to the terrace, straight to Mr Franklin, ignoring Mr Godfrey, who stepped back and left them alone. I watched Miss Rachel's words bring a look of complete astonishment to Mr Franklin's face. Seeing my lady join them on the terrace, Miss Rachel said some quick last words to her cousin and rushed inside. Mr Godfrey joined my lady and Mr Franklin and they walked off, Mr Franklin explaining something. Inside, Miss Rachel brushed past Seegrave on her way upstairs. 'I don't want to talk to you!' she cried, a wild, angry look in her eyes. 'My diamond is lost. Neither you nor anybody else will ever find it!'

I accompanied Seegrave upstairs. Miss Rachel's bedroom door was locked. We heard her crying inside. The police officer was losing his patience. He asked to see the servants. They were questioned one by one, including Penelope for a second time. My daughter's anger had made a bad impression on him. Afterwards, she rushed out teary-eyed saying that he had as good as told her that she had taken the jewel!

Seegrave then searched the servants' rooms, and found nothing. While he was deciding on his next line of action, Mr Franklin asked to see me in the library. Rosanna rushed out as I entered. The library had been cleaned in the morning, so she had no business in there. Red-faced, with a strange, self-important look in her eyes, she said, 'Mr Franklin dropped a ring upstairs. I gave it to him,' and walked away.

I found Mr Franklin writing. 'Please send this telegraph, Betteredge,' he said. 'My father knows the Commissioner of Police. I hope he can send us a cleverer head than Seegrave's.' He lowered his voice to a whisper. 'I think Rosanna Spearman may know more about the Moonstone than she ought to – or she's gone a bit weak in the head. She certainly behaved very strangely just now. She came in and she said: "They'll never find the diamond, will they, sir? Or the person who took it. I'll make sure of that." She actually nodded and smiled at me! I was about to ask her what she meant when you knocked.'

Passing the kitchen with the telegram I saw all the servants were at dinner except Rosanna. I was told she had suddenly felt ill and had gone upstairs. 'Curious,' I said. 'She looked well enough just now.' Penelope followed me out. 'Don't talk like that, father!' she whispered. 'They'll only treat her even worse. The poor girl is breaking her heart over Mr Franklin.'

Seegrave now had a different theory: someone in the house must have helped the Indians. Mr Franklin offered to take him into town to question them again. Mr Godfrey, interested, asked to go with them. Before they left, Mr Franklin had a word with me. 'I won't send the telegram until we've seen the Indians,' he said. 'And keep an eye on Rosanna Spearman while I'm away. And Miss Rachel. I'm very worried about her.' He left me suddenly.

Rosanna came down to tea looking ill, was given some medicine and went back upstairs. Miss Rachel remained in her room, saying she was unwell. The gentlemen returned before dinner. Mr Murthwaite had kindly acted as interpreter, but the interview had failed to throw any new light on the affair. Mr Franklin had sent his telegram, and Superintendent Seegrave was going to return the following morning.

Chapter 9   Sergeant Cuff Arrives

Two pieces of news came on Friday morning. First, the baker had met Rosanna walking towards Fritzinghall on Thursday afternoon; second, Dr Candy had caught a cold in the rain and had a dangerously high fever.

Shortly after Seegrave arrived, a telegram came for Mr Franklin. 'Sergeant Cuff is arriving this morning!' he said. 'There isn't a mystery this man can't solve!' Seegrave sat down immediately to write a report for the famous London detective. I was watching him anxiously chewing on his pen, when I saw a miserable-looking figure dressed in black arrive at the gates outside. At first sight, the bony little old man seemed almost like a ghost. Could *this* be the famous Sergeant Cuff?

Outside, as he introduced himself in a quiet, sad voice, his steely grey eyes met mine. They were as sharp as knives, those eyes, and seemed to know more about you than you did yourself. I told him Superintendent Seegrave was waiting to see him and he followed me silently towards the house. The first sign of any interest that he showed was when he saw our rose garden. He began talking to the gardener – who soon found out he was an expert on roses. He touched a white rose with his thin yellow fingers. 'Pretty dear,' he said softly, as though speaking to a child.

Seegrave and Cuff spoke in private in my office. Afterwards, the Superintendent seemed excited and the Sergeant was yawning. 'The Sergeant wishes to see Miss Verinder's sitting-room,' Seegrave announced authoritatively. I took them upstairs.

Softly, Cuff examined the cabinet and the entire room. Only the door seemed to awaken his curiosity. 'How did this happen?' he asked me, placing a stick-like finger on the dried smear. Seegrave answered: 'The servants crowded into the room yesterday morning. A dress did it. I ordered them out.'

'Did either of you notice which dress?' asked Cuff, still speaking to me. 'I can't remember,' Seegrave replied. 'It's unimportant.' Cuff gave Seegrave a sad look. 'In all my experience of this dirty little world I have never known anything unimportant. We must find the dress that did this; and we must know when that paint was wet.' He turned to me. 'Sir, yesterday, you all came in here around eleven, I believe. Does anybody know whether the paint was dry at that time?' I told him Mr Franklin knew. Cuff sent for him and he joined us in the room. 'The paint dries in twelve hours,' he declared. 'The smeared part was finished at 3 p.m. on Wednesday.'

'Therefore, Mr Blake, the paint dried around 3 a.m. on Thursday. It must have been dry for approximately eight hours when you all came in here at eleven.' Miss Rachel suddenly rushed out of her room. Cuff bowed and introduced himself. 'Take my advice, Sergeant,' she said angrily. 'Don't allow Mr Franklin Blake to help you.' She turned to Mr Franklin with a wild look but, curiously, was unable to look him in the eyes. Cuff's eyes never left her. 'Thank you, miss,' he said. 'Do *you* know anything about the smear? Might you have done it by accident?'

'I know nothing,' she declared and went and shut herself up in her room again. Hearing her burst out crying inside, Cuff said: 'Miss Verinder is extremely upset about the loss of her diamond.' A faint smile appeared on his lips. 'Naturally! – it's an extremely valuable jewel.' His face hardened. 'Now, we must discover when the paint was last seen without that smear. Who saw it last on Wednesday night?'

24

Only the door seemed to awaken his curiosity. 'How did this happen?' he asked me, placing a stick-like finger on the dried smear.

'Possibly Mr Betteredge's daughter, Penelope,' Mr Franklin replied. Cuff took me aside. 'We don't want to annoy the servants, do we?' he said, 'so please tell them I don't suspect anybody. I have no evidence – yet – that the diamond has been stolen. I only know it's been lost. Say I simply want them to help me find it. Now go and fetch your daughter.'

Cuff seemed to approve of Penelope. She told him she saw them finish the last part, and had seen it as late as midnight, without a smear. She had been careful not to touch it. He examined her dress. There was no trace of paint. He then asked me whether a dog might have entered the room. I said this was impossible. He studied the smear closely and was satisfied it had been made by clothing – between midnight and three o'clock on Thursday morning. 'Yes, Superintendent,' he said, 'Please feel free to return to Fritzinghall. But leave one of your men here, will you? – in case I need him. Good morning.' He went to the window and stood there whistling 'The Last Rose of Summer.'

Seegrave, deeply offended, marched noisily out. Nodding thoughtfully, his eyes on Miss Rachel's bedroom door, Cuff asked to speak to my lady. Leaving the room I heard Mr Franklin say to him, 'Can you guess yet who has stolen the diamond?'

'*Nobody has stolen the diamond,*' Cuff replied.

Chapter 10   The Search Begins

'*Must* I see him?' my lady said. 'I don't know why but I have a feeling that horrible little man is bringing trouble and misery into this house. But if I must see him, I must. Stay with me while we talk, will you, Gabriel?'

Mr Franklin returned to Mr Godfrey who was soon to be

leaving. I took Cuff to my lady's room. 'At present, only one thing is certain,' he said to her. 'The diamond is missing.' He explained the smear on the door. 'The stained dress may lead us to the stone,' he said in conclusion. 'So I must search the servants' wardrobes, I'm afraid.' She refused, saying she would not let them be insulted a second time. 'I don't think they'll object, your ladyship,' he replied, 'if I tell them − with your permission − that I'm going to search *everybody's* wardrobes.'

She seemed to appreciate the Sergeant's clever solution. 'Very well, I agree to let you search my room. I am sure Miss Verinder, Mr Blake, and Mr Ablewhite won't refuse either.' Mr Godfrey came in to say goodbye with Mr Franklin. My lady explained the Sergeant's plan. Mr Franklin agreed to let his wardrobe be searched. Mr Godfrey offered the Sergeant the keys to his luggage, saying it could be searched and sent on to London later. Mr Godfrey left a message for Miss Rachel − which made it clear to me that he had not taken her No for an answer.

'My lady,' said Cuff as soon as the young gentlemen had left, 'I must be able to account for the clothes in the house, especially the clothes that have been washed. They will be recorded in the washing book, I believe?' Rosanna brought in the washing book, looking very tired and pale, and left. He examined the book, shut it again, and said, 'The last time I saw the woman who brought this book she was in prison for theft.'

I told him the truth about Rosanna. My lady made it very clear how satisfied she was with her. 'You don't suspect her, I hope?' she added, getting up to go and ask Miss Rachel for the keys to her wardrobe. The Sergeant bowed. 'I have said, your ladyship, that I don't suspect anyone of stealing − at least not at the moment.'

Cuff whistled 'The Last Rose of Summer', until Samuel

came in with a note. Miss Rachel flatly refused to let her wardrobe be searched. 'Ah!' said the Sergeant, as though somehow expecting this. 'It's all wardrobes or none – a pity.' His sad eyes fell on me. 'You don't seem too disappointed,' I said. 'Mr Betteredge,' he replied, 'let's go and have a look at those roses, shall we?'

Chapter 11   Rosanna

'Walls have ears,' said Cuff, examining a rose. 'In my business we prefer the open air, like this beauty.' He sighed. 'I've decided to search the servants' thoughts and actions instead of their wardrobes. But before I do, can I ask you whether any of them have acted strangely since the loss of the diamond?' Rosanna immediately came to mind, but before I could answer I saw Cuff's eyes suddenly look towards the bushes. 'What's the matter?' I asked. 'Oh, just a pain in my back,' he replied loudly, as though wanting a third person to hear. We went on to the terrace. 'Does young Rosanna have a lover?' he asked. 'If she hasn't, she's behaving suspiciously. She was hiding in the bushes just now.'

The bushy path by the rose garden was Mr Franklin's favourite walk. He would take it on his way back from the station. Many times, Penelope had seen Rosanna hanging about there since his arrival. I explained this to the Sergeant, and told him that the poor girl was in love with Mr Franklin. 'I'm glad – it explains things,' he said. 'And no doubt he hasn't even noticed the girl?'

'Yes, Sergeant,' I said. 'I'm afraid ugly women have a bad time in this world.' He looked me very hard in the face, then took my hand and shook it. 'Mr Betteredge,' he said, 'I like you.'

Back in my office, he asked me to call the servants one by one. The cook was the first, then my lady's maid, then Penelope. Rosanna was next. She stayed longer than any of them and came out as pale as death. Samuel followed; Nancy was last. When she had left I went into Cuff's 'courtroom' and found him whistling 'The Last Rose of Summer'. 'If Rosanna asks to go out,' he said, 'let the poor thing go. But tell me first.' The cook entered. Rosanna had asked to go out for some air because she had a headache. I said yes. As soon as the cook had gone I showed Cuff the servants' entrance and he disappeared.

I had a chat with the cook and my lady's maid. Neither of them believed Rosanna had been ill the previous day. They had knocked on her door several times during the afternoon. No answer; and it was locked. They had seen a light under the door at midnight, heard the sounds of a fire at four in the morning – in June! And of course they had told Cuff all this.

Later, out in the afternoon, I met Mr Franklin on the bushy path. When he had returned, my lady had told him about Miss Rachel's refusal of the search. I told him everything else that had happened. 'Rosanna Spearman went to Fritzinghall secretly,' he said. 'She burnt her paint-stained dress. She must have stolen the diamond. I must tell my aunt immediately.'

'Not just yet, please, sir,' said Cuff's sad voice behind us. We turned to him.

'Why not just yet?' said Mr Franklin, annoyed.

'Because, sir, if you tell her ladyship, she will tell Miss Verinder.'

Mr Franklin walked up to the Sergeant and stared threateningly down at him. 'Are you forbidding me?' he enquired.

'I'm saying, sir, that if you tell Lady Verinder or anyone else before I give you permission I will abandon the case.' Realizing he had no choice, Mr Franklin turned away angrily and left us.

'Mr Betteredge,' Cuff said, 'please leave the detective work to me, will you?' He took my arm. 'What do you want of me now?' I said. 'Information, as usual,' he replied with a weak smile. He pointed towards the Shivering Sand. 'Show me the beach.'

As we approached the bay in the grey of evening, Cuff said, 'I understand your charitable feelings for that poor girl. But she's not in the slightest danger of getting into trouble – not if I can prove she was simply concerned with the *disappearance* of the diamond. I have evidence – as plain as the nose on your face – that she's simply an instrument in the hands of another person.'

'Can't you give that person a name?' I said.

'Can't you, Mr Betteredge?' I shook my head. He gave me one of his sad looks. 'She went secretly to Fritzinghall yesterday to buy cloth to make a dress exactly the same as the stained one. The fire in her room was to heat the iron to press the new dress, not to burn the stained one. She knows that the cook and Lady Verinder's maid suspect her, so she still has to hide the dress, doesn't she?' I nodded. 'I followed her this evening to the fishing village, to a cottage. She came out with something hidden under her coat. I followed her north along the coast as far as I could – unfortunately there's nowhere to hide along there. I hope we'll meet her by coming round this way. If not, the sand may tell us what she's been doing.'

I felt suddenly uneasy. I could hear Rosanna telling me that the quicksand seemed to be pulling her to it against her will. The light was rapidly fading and, as there often is when the tide is about to turn, an awful, breathless calm hung over the bay. Cold fear ran up my spine as we saw the mirror-like surface of the sand begin to tremble. 'A most murderous place,' said the Sergeant, echoing my thoughts.

'And no sign of her anywhere.' We went down on to the beach.

'The only way to get here from the fishing village is by coming round below the cliffs at low tide,' I said. We had walked south a hundred yards when Cuff suddenly kneeled. 'A woman's,' he said, examining footprints in the sand. They went round in circles then finally into the water. 'She was obviously trying to hide where her walk ended, to hide whatever she had under her coat. Perhaps if we go to the cottage we may find out what it was.'

We reached the fishing village before dark. The cottage belonged to a family called Yolland. The daughter, Lucy, who had a deformed foot, had made friends with Rosanna. Mrs Yolland invited us in. The fisherman and his son were out. Lucy, always tired and weak, was upstairs. Cuff showed wonderful patience, casually bringing the talk round to Rosanna. He assured her that his only aim was to clear Rosanna of unfair accusations by the other servants concerning the Moonstone. 'They hated the poor girl!' Mrs Yolland interrupted. 'She said she was going to leave – very soon.'

'I see,' said Cuff sadly. 'So she has no other friends – apart from you?'

'Oh, yes!' replied Mrs Yolland. 'This evening, she went upstairs on her own. "I want to write to a friend," she said. And later she bought some things she needed for travelling. She showed us a metal case. We had two of these. I sold her one. Sailors use them for keeping things dry. And I sold her two chains.' Softly, Cuff began whistling 'The Last Rose of Summer'.

Chapter 12   Rachel's Decision

'Yes,' said Cuff as we left the village in the dark, 'she joined the chains to the case and sunk it in the water or in the quicksand, fixing it to the rocks. All very clear, but — the mystery is, what is in the case? Not the diamond, obviously.' Not the diamond? I thought. The stained dress then? He stopped and turned to me in the shadows. 'Does anything that is thrown into that quicksand ever come out again?'

'Never,' I answered.

'The question is why,' Cuff continued. 'Why not just tie the dress around a heavy stone and throw it into the quicksand? But is it a dress? Could it be a nightgown, for example? I must go to Fritzinghall tomorrow and find out what she bought.'

When we got back, the servants were at supper. Rosanna had returned an hour before, had gone upstairs to take off her coat and was now sitting quietly with them. I followed Cuff round to the back of the house. He looked up at Miss Rachel's bedroom window, watching lights passing to and fro. 'I bet you a pound, Mr Betteredge,' he said, 'that an hour ago Miss Verinder decided to leave the house.'

Samuel met us inside. 'Her ladyship is waiting to see you and Sergeant Cuff,' he said. 'How long has she been waiting?' asked Cuff. 'An hour, sir,' Samuel replied.

As I knocked on my lady's door, Cuff whispered, 'I shouldn't be surprised if there's a disturbance in the house tonight.'

Only a small lamp was on in the room. 'Sergeant,' said my lady from the shadows, 'Miss Verinder decided about an hour ago to go and stay with her aunt, Mrs Ablewhite, in Fritzinghall. She will be leaving tomorrow morning.'

'Might it be possible, my lady, to persuade her to delay

leaving a little? I have to go to Fritzinghall tomorrow morning, and won't be back until 2 p.m. I would like to say a few words to her − unexpectedly − before she goes.' Unwillingly, my lady accepted. She told me to tell the carriage not to come until two. 'And please don't mention me as the cause for putting off her departure,' Cuff added. My lady was about to say something, but stopped herself. She waved her hand for us to leave her.

'She almost told us,' Cuff said once we were outside, 'and the mystery that puzzles you would have been at an end tonight.'

'Curse you!' I cried. 'There's something you've known all this time! Tell me the truth, Sergeant, what do you suspect?'

'I don't suspect. I know,' he said calmly.

'Are you trying to tell me she stole her own diamond?' I said.

'She has had it all the time, calculating that we will suspect Rosanna.' He almost smiled. 'We'll let the matter rest tonight, I think. I'm hungry. Would you like to have supper with me?'

I said I'd lost my appetite, left him with the gardener and went out for some air. Dark clouds were gathering in the distance; the wind was rising; bad weather was on the way. Samuel brought me a note from my lady. The judge in Fritzinghall had written to remind her that the three Indians were to be released early in the coming week. If we had any more questions to ask them there was no time to lose. When I got back inside, Cuff and the gardener were arguing about roses over a bottle of whisky. He read the message, searched his mind a moment, said, 'I believe there is a gentleman in Fritzinghall who is an expert on Indian matters,' then returned to the argument.

I met Penelope in the passage outside. She had been helping

Miss Rachel pack. Apparently, when her mother had told her that her departure had to be delayed, she had been violently angry. Her mother, equally angry with Miss Rachel, went to her, whispered something in her ear, and Rachel left the room. Miss Rachel's bell rang while we were talking and Penelope left me.

Later, as I was putting the lights out, I couldn't help feeling that some terrible threat was hanging over us all. Upstairs, in front of Miss Rachel's rooms, I found Cuff lying asleep on three chairs put together across the corridor. 'What are you doing here?' I asked.

'Whatever Rosanna may have hidden, it was clear to me that Miss Rachel couldn't go away until she knew it was hidden. The two of them must have communicated tonight. If they try again, I want to be in the way.'

Chapter 13   A Letter

Next morning, Cuff didn't leave for Fritzinghall straight away as expected. I met Mr Franklin on his favourite walk down the bushy path. The Sergeant joined us. 'What do you want?' Mr Franklin said to him sharply. 'I want to remind you, sir,' Cuff replied, 'that I am an officer of the law and it is your duty to give me any special information which you possess.'

'I have no *special* information, and have nothing to say.'

'Not even about Rosanna Spearman?' said Cuff. 'Hasn't she spoken to you, or tried to speak to you?' As Cuff said this Rosanna appeared nearby. Penelope was with her, obviously trying to make her go back inside. Seeing Mr Franklin, Rosanna stopped. Cuff, pretending not to notice them, said loudly, 'You needn't be afraid of harming the girl, sir.'

'I take no interest in Rosanna Spearman,' Mr Franklin replied. Hearing this, Rosanna turned away. She let my daughter take her by the hand and lead her inside. 'I shall go to Fritzinghall now, Mr Betteredge,' Cuff said quietly. 'Expect me back at two.'

After breakfast, after Mr Franklin had left for a long walk in the rain, Penelope came to me. 'Please talk to Rosanna, father,' she said. 'I'm so worried about her. Mr Franklin has hurt her cruelly without intending it.' I asked her why she was in the garden. 'She wanted to speak to him,' she replied. 'I tried to stop her. I told her she was stupid to expect him to take any interest in her. She frightened me, father. She turned to stone when he said those words. Since then she's gone around in a kind of dream.'

We found her sweeping a corridor. There was a strange dullness in her eyes. 'Cheer up, Rosanna!' I said. 'If you've got something on your mind you can tell me. I'm your friend.' She went on sweeping, more like a machine than a living person.

'Yes,' she said, 'I will tell – but Mr Franklin, not you. But I shan't trouble him today.'

'You can tell me, if it will relieve your mind,' said Penelope.

'No,' she said to herself, 'I know a better way of relieving my mind.' We left her as we had found her, like a woman in a dream. She should see a doctor, I thought, then remembered that Dr Candy was extremely ill. There was his strange assistant, Ezra Jennings, but I – and no one else – trusted him.

Cuff returned at ten to two. 'I saw the Indians with Mr Murthwaite,' he said. 'They will be set free on Wednesday. There is no doubt that they came here to steal the Moonstone, but I am equally sure they have nothing to do with the loss of

35

the jewel. One thing is certain, Mr Betteredge: if we don't find it, they will.' Mr Franklin, returning, passed us in silence. 'Rosanna bought a length of plain cloth,' said Cuff, 'enough to make a nightgown. Plain cloth means servant's cloth. But why, having made the replacement, does she hide the smeared nightgown instead of destroying it? There is only one way of finding out if she won't tell us. We must search the Shivering Sand.'

Samuel arrived with Miss Rachel's carriage at two. 'When you leave,' said Cuff, 'you'll see a man waiting among the trees by the gates. He'll jump up on the back of the carriage. All right?'

My lady came out, said nothing to me or Cuff, and stood stiffly waiting for her daughter. Rachel came downstairs, colourless, her eyes bright and fierce. She kissed her mother hurriedly, said, 'Try to forgive me, mamma,' and ran to the carriage. Cuff jumped in front of her. 'What do you want?' she said angrily.

'Your leaving makes it extremely difficult for me to find the diamond,' said Cuff. She got in and ordered the carriage to leave. My lady, in sorrow and shame, turned to go inside, nearly bumping into Mr Franklin as he ran down the steps. 'Goodbye, Rachel!' he shouted, waving. 'Drive on!' Miss Rachel shouted to Samuel. Mr Franklin called after my lady as the carriage drove away: 'Aunt! You were right. Now I must leave. Thank you for all your kindness.' Tears in her eyes, my lady went inside.

Mr Franklin turned to me. 'Please, Betteredge, get me to the station,' he said and went inside. 'It's time to sort this business out,' said Cuff. 'Where's Rosanna Spearman?'

We asked servants. She hadn't been seen for an hour. 'Your dear Rosanna won't slip through my fingers that easily,' he said. 'She and Miss Rachel will meet at Fritzinghall. She's either gone there – before I can get there – or she's gone to the Shivering Sand.'

Nancy, the kitchen maid, said she had seen Rosanna stop the butcher, who had just delivered meat to the house, and ask him to post a letter. The butcher had said it was a complicated way to send a letter to the fishing village, that it wouldn't get there until Monday. Rosanna had said that it didn't matter how long it took to arrive and the butcher had driven away with it. 'Well?' I asked when we were alone again. 'The hiding-place is in that letter,' Cuff replied. 'I shall pay Mrs Yolland another visit on Monday.'

Chapter 14   The Shivering Sands

Duffy, the gardener's boy, had seen Rosanna half an hour before, running towards the sea. 'Come with me, Duffy,' said Cuff. 'And you, Mr Betteredge, stay here till I come back.' They hurried off towards the Shivering Sand, but not long afterwards Duffy came running back. I had to send one of Rosanna's shoes quickly. I sent him back to say I would follow with the shoe. Fifteen minutes later, I reached the shore. Dark clouds were rushing low overhead. The sea was thundering at the mouth of the bay, sending great waves rolling in over the sand. Cuff was alone on the beach. Hearing me approach behind him, he turned. There was a look of horror in his eyes. He grabbed the shoe out of my hand and placed it in a footmark in the sand. It fitted exactly.

We followed the footprints to the mouth of the bay. They went into the water at a place where the rocks and the sand joined. Seconds earlier the rising tide had wiped them out. We looked everywhere for footsteps coming back towards land until the rising water forced us to stop. Cuff stared out over the

I could no longer feel the driving rain, all I could hear was Rosanna telling me that the sands seemed to be pulling her to a watery grave.

waters rushing in deeper and deeper over the whole face of the quicksand. There was a look of defeat on his face. 'A fatal accident has happened to her on those rocks,' he said. I could no longer feel the driving rain, all I could hear was her telling me that the sands seemed to be pulling her to a watery grave. The horror of it struck me. Gently, Cuff led me away from where she had died. Yolland ran up to us. He looked down at Rosanna's footprints dissolving in the rain. 'Is there any chance of finding her when the tide turns?' asked the Sergeant. 'None,' said the fisherman. 'What the sand gets, the sand keeps for ever.'

On our way back, Duffy ran up to us with a note. 'Penelope found this in Rosanna's room,' he said. Tears came to my eyes as I read it:

Mr Betteredge, when you next see the Shivering Sand, please try and forgive me. Yes, I found my grave there. I died grateful for your kindness.

Rosanna Spearman

The note had thrown the whole house into a state of panic. As we passed my lady's door, she threw it open violently, with a horrified look on her face. Mr Franklin was trying to calm her. 'This is your fault!' she shouted at Cuff. 'Gabriel, give this miserable person his money and remove him from my sight!'

'I will accept your dismissal, but not your money,' Cuff replied. 'I am paid for doing my duty – which is not yet done,' Oddly, my lady seemed almost embarrassed by his flat professional manner. He went on: 'When I have told you plainly, your ladyship, what action must be taken to get back the Moonstone, my responsibilities will have ended,' After a moment's thought, my lady signalled Cuff and me to follow her back into her room.

'Your ladyship,' said Cuff when we had sat down. 'I believe some unbearable anxiety concerning the diamond drove

Rosanna to suicide. And I believe your daughter can tell us whether this is true.' My lady took her cheque book, looked at Cuff steadily and said, 'You suspect Miss Verinder of deceiving us by hiding the diamond for some purpose of her own?'

'That is it, my lady.'

'I know my daughter, Sergeant, and I can tell you she is *absolutely incapable* of doing what you suspect.' She sighed, controlling herself. 'Nevertheless, I give you permission to go on and explain yourself.'

'Thank you,' said Cuff. 'But I must be frank, your ladyship. It has been my experience that young ladies of Miss Verinder's social position can have debts which they dare not admit to their nearest relatives and friends. Events and behaviour in this house suggest this to me. Miss Verinder is still extremely upset more than twenty-four hours after losing her diamond; she has developed a sudden strange dislike for Mr Blake, the Superintendent and myself – the three people who have been most actively trying to find her jewel; and, of course, she refuses to cooperate. Her behaviour tells me she has debts and has pawned the diamond to pay them.' He continued, unbothered by our shocked silence. 'That is the case against her. Now, what is the case against her and the dead Rosanna Spearman together? As soon as I saw Rosanna I suspected her of being involved. It was a cleverly planned conspiracy – from Miss Verinder's point of view. Better than leading us to think that the Moonstone was simply lost, she could trick us into believing it was stolen – by a woman with a criminal record. Poor dead Rosanna was the ideal person to help her pawn the stone privately. She knew one of the few men in London who could advance a large sum of money on such a famous jewel – without asking questions. I will now tell you what I propose to do. I intend to watch Miss Verinder closely. And I shall send one of my men to make an arrangement with that money-lender in London – you can be sure Rosanna gave his name to Miss Verinder. Would you agree to this?'

'No,' said my lady flatly.

Cuff went on, undiscouraged. 'Another way, my lady, would be to tell Miss Verinder, without warning, of Rosanna's death. Sudden sorrow may encourage her to admit everything. Would you agree to this?' To my astonishment my lady nodded. 'Then, my lady,' said Cuff, getting up, 'I wish you good morning.' My lady raised her hand. 'Sergeant, I feel it would be better if I told her. *I* will go to Fritzinghall. You may rely on me to try the experiment.' As soon as my lady had left, I informed Mr Franklin of her decision. He decided to wait for the news from Fritzinghall before leaving. I returned to Cuff. He was studying his diary. 'I was seeing what my next professional appointment is,' he said.

'You think it's all over?' I said.

'I think Lady Verinder is an extremely clever woman. Now, where is that gardener? I promised to teach him something about roses before I left.'

My lady's carriage returned earlier than expected. She had decided to stay at her sister's in Fritzinghall for the time being. The driver brought two letters, one for Mr Franklin, one for me. A cheque dropped out of mine when I opened it. The Sergeant appeared on the steps. 'Ah!' he said in his sad way. 'News from her ladyship?' I read him the letter:

Gabriel, Miss Verinder declared that she has never spoken a private word to Rosanna or communicated with her by other means. They never met, not even accidentally, on the night the diamond was lost. I warned her that her behaviour was inviting suspicion. She assured me that she has no debts to anybody, and that the diamond has never been in her possession since she put it in the drawer on Wednesday night. She remained stubbornly silent when I asked her if she could explain the

41

stone's disappearance. Tears in her eyes, she said, 'The day will come
when you will know why I'm silent.'

Give Sergeant Cuff this cheque and tell him that I am absolutely
certain that his suspicions are mistaken.

Cuff's eyebrows went up when he looked at the cheque. 'I
will always remember her ladyship's generosity,' he said, but he
placed it on the table. 'A fine woman. Yes, Lady Verinder has
smoothed things over very cleverly – for the moment. But we
shall hear more of the Moonstone before too long.'

'If you don't think Miss Rachel is telling the truth then prove
it,' I said angrily. I was sick of his accusations. He was so
obviously wrong. Miss Rachel was incapable of doing what
he suspected.

He wasn't offended. Quite the opposite – he took my hand
and shook it! 'You're a fine man, sir!' he said warmly. 'I won't say
a word more about Lady Verinder and her daughter. I'll simply
say that these three things will happen. First, you will hear from
the Yollands – after Rosanna's letter is delivered on Monday.
Second, you will hear of the three Indians again – here, if Miss
Rachel remains here, in London if she goes to London. And
third, sooner or later you will hear from Mr Septimus Luker, a
money-lender. Time will tell if I am right or wrong, Mr
Betteredge, and if we don't meet again before I retire from
this dirty job, I hope you'll come and visit me at my cottage
near London. And bring the gardener – I'll teach that man
a thing or two about roses!'

I couldn't help liking the man, even though I hated him.

Chapter 15   To London

Mr Franklin had made up his mind to leave. 'Wait a day or two longer, sir, and give Miss Rachel another chance,' I said. He handed me my lady's letter.

Franklin, I am forced to believe now that the Moonstone's mysterious disappearance is no mystery to Rachel. I have tried everything but something forbids her from breaking her silence. She is in a pitiful state of nervous excitement. I shall take her to London for a change of air and some medical advice. Please come and see us there, will you? But not straight away. It is impossible to reason with her at the moment, and for the moment you two are better apart. Give her time.

'The Moonstone has given Colonel Herncastle his revenge,' said Mr Franklin. 'But in a way he never dreamt of.' We said goodbye and, sad and weary, I went inside. He was right. The diamond had brought us nothing but unhappiness.

The next day (Sunday) Samuel brought a message. My lady and Miss Rachel were leaving directly from Fritzinghall for London that day. Penelope was to accompany them but I was to remain in the country.

I had said goodbye to Penelope at the gates and was walking back through the rose garden when I heard my name called. I turned and saw Limping Lucy. 'Where's Franklin Blake?' she said fiercely, '*Mr* Franklin Blake, you mean,' I replied. '*Murderer* Franklin Blake, I mean,' she shouted. '*He* caused her death!'

'What makes you say such a thing?' I replied angrily.

'You don't care!' she said softly. 'Everybody treated her badly. Except me. I loved her.' Tears came to her eyes. 'I'd saved up a little money. We were going to go and live together in London and earn our living by sewing. Until *he* came. She lost her mind when that man arrived. "I can't live without him," and "Oh,

Lucy, he never even looks at me." It was pitiful. And then her letter came this morning.' Wiping her eyes, she cried, 'Where is he?'

'He's in London,' I replied. 'Why do you want to see him?'

'I have a letter from Rosanna to give him. If he wants it he must come back and get it from me. I and nobody else must give it to him.' She turned and limped away towards the Shivering Sand.

On Tuesday morning a letter came from Mr Franklin's father's head servant, an old friend of mine. He mentioned that Mr Franklin had left England for Europe on Sunday morning. And so, for some time to come, there would be no hope of knowing whether Rosanna's letter contained a confession or not.

Thursday brought news from Penelope. A London doctor had earned a lot of money by suggesting that the best cure for Miss Rachel was amusement: flower shows, operas, dances, that sort of thing. Mr Godfrey had visited and was most politely received.

Saturday's post brought an envelope from Cuff containing an article from a London newspaper, a report from the law courts:

Mr Septimus Luker, a dealer in Oriental jewellery, complained to the court that he had been annoyed by three poor Indians. Again and again they had tried to enter his house, asking for charity. Mr Luker believed they intended to rob him and demanded that they should be arrested. The judge dismissed the complaint, saying there was no evidence. He advised Mr Luker to get the police's advice on how to protect his property.

The devilish Indian diamond had left us and found its way to London. And so it is here that I must leave the story for someone else to take up.

PART 2   THE DISCOVERY OF THE
TRUTH (1848–1849)

FIRST NARRATIVE

by Miss Clack, niece of the late Sir John Verinder

Chapter 1   A Strange Mistake

My dear parents (both now in heaven) taught me to fold my
clothes carefully, to always say my prayers before going to bed,
and to keep a diary. The last of these excellent habits will, I hope,
enable me to be useful to a wealthy relation. Recently, Mr
Franklin Blake wrote to me here in France (where I have
been forced to live for economic reasons). He asked me – with
the typical lack of feeling of the rich – to reopen wounds that
Time has hardly closed. He offered me a small sum to write a
narrative of what I witnessed while visiting Aunt Verinder in
London. After much searching of my soul I decided that it
was my Christian duty to swallow my pride, accept his cheque,
and help him.

◆

My diary tells me I was accidentally passing Aunt Verinder's
house in Montagu Square on July 3rd 1848, and felt that
it would be polite to knock. The daughter of that godless
old devil Betteredge answered the door. She informed me
that Aunt Verinder and her daughter (I really cannot call her
my cousin!) had arrived a week before. I sent her upstairs to
say that I didn't want to disturb them but as I was passing I
wondered whether I could be of any use to them. When the
Betteredge girl came downstairs I decided to have a Christian
word with her about the unnecessary amount of ribbons on
her cap. She opened the front door before telling me (with a

45

minimum of politeness) that I was invited to lunch tomorrow. I left.

That evening we had a meeting of the Young Mothers' Small Clothes Society. I was a member of the charity's Committee, as was my precious and most admirable friend, Mr Godfrey Ablewhite. To my disappointment he did not appear that night, and I was shocked to hear from my Christian sisters of the Committee that the previous Friday he and a gentleman called Mr Septimus Luker had been victims of a strange conspiracy.

According to the newspapers, early on June 30th our gifted Mr Ablewhite, after cashing a cheque at a bank in Lombard Street, passed Mr Luker – a perfect stranger – who happened to be leaving the bank at the same time. The stranger insisted on Mr Godfrey leaving first, and the two men went their separate ways. Mr Godfrey went back to his house in Lambeth, where a poorly dressed young boy was waiting for him. The boy handed him a letter, saying he had been asked to deliver it by an old lady he didn't know. It asked him to go, an hour later, to a house in Northumberland Street. The woman, who intended to give a large sum of money to charity, wanted information on the Young Mothers' Small Clothes Society. Our Christian Hero never hesitates when good can be done. He went instantly.

A very respectable-looking Englishman answered the door and led him to an apartment at the back of the house. Entering, Mr Godfrey noticed an ancient Oriental book on the table. As he was admiring it, a brown-skinned arm took him by the neck. He struggled but there was more than one person. His eyes were bandaged, he was tied to a chair, and was searched. Words were spoken in a foreign tongue, then the men left.

He was discovered later by the owners of the house. They had rented the apartment to the Englishman the day before. Seeing that the door had been left open for a long time they went in to see if anything was wrong. Mr Godfrey's belongings were lying everywhere but nothing was missing. The Oriental book was gone. Had Mr Godfrey been the victim of a strange mistake?

Later that day the same thing happened again. Mr Luker, having left the bank, visited various parts of London on business. Returning home, he found a letter waiting for him. A customer from Manchester, a collector of Oriental antiques, announced that he was on a short visit to London and desired to see Mr Luker urgently about an important sale. He drove immediately to an address in Tottenham Court Road where exactly the same thing happened to him – with one slight difference. Mr Luker's gold watch, his wallet, nothing was missing except one thing: a receipt for an extremely valuable object which he had put in the bank. The receipt was useless to anyone else since it clearly stated that only Mr Luker himself could remove the object from the bank.

Mr Luker hurried to the bank. Nobody had been there with the receipt. He went to the police who told him about Mr Godfrey's similar experience. They believed that a robbery had been planned and that one of the thieves had seen Mr Godfrey accidentally speaking to Mr Luker.

♦

On Tuesday, dear Aunt Verinder received me with her usual kindness. However, I soon noticed that something was wrong. Anxious looks kept escaping her in the direction of her daughter who, as usual, disappointed me – how could such a plain-looking person be the child of such fine parents? After lunch, she got up in her shamefully colourful dress and said, 'I'll go and read now, mamma, but tell me if Godfrey calls. I can't wait to hear all about his adventure in Northumberland Street.' She gave me a careless look. 'Goodbye, Clack,' she said and left in a cloud of perfume. I refused to let her make me angry. I did what any good Christian would do: I simply decided to pray for her that night.

When we were alone my aunt told me the whole story of the Indian diamond and of Rachel's worrying behaviour. None of it surprised *me* – I have known Rachel since she was a child. The one thing that did shock me was Aunt Verinder's decision to have a doctor examine her. The poor girl was more in need of God's help! 'This strange adventure of Godfrey's has happened at the wrong time,' said my aunt. 'Rachel has been restless and excited ever since she heard about it.'

'Dear aunt,' I said. 'She's obviously keeping a sinful secret from you and everybody. Something in these recent events threatens her with discovery.' There was a knock on the door. Miss Cap Ribbons entered and announced a visitor, Mr Godfrey Ablewhite.

Chapter 2   Rumours and Reputations

A model of manners, Mr Godfrey walked in shortly after the announcement of his name. We both asked him whether he felt himself again after his terrible adventure. 'My dear aunt, my dear Miss Clack!' he exclaimed, 'What have I done to deserve all this sympathy? I would have preferred to have kept the whole thing to myself!' I was overcome by the heavenly gentleness of his smile, by the richness of his deep voice. 'And how is dear Rachel?' he enquired. 'And you, Miss Clack, I really do hope to be able to be at the Young Mothers' Small Clothes meeting next week.' I was about to reply when we were disturbed by Rachel.

'I am charmed to see you, Godfrey,' she said. 'I wish you had brought Mr Luker with you. Never mind, tell me the whole story immediately.' I was sad to see him take her hand. 'Dearest Rachel,' he said, 'The newspapers have told it better than I can.'

'Rachel, darling,' I remarked, 'true greatness and courage are always modest.'

'Godfrey,' she said, not taking any notice of me, 'I am sure you are not great and I am certain that if you ever had any modesty your lady-admirers took it from you years ago. You have a reason for not talking about your adventure and I will find it out.'

'My reason is simple,' he answered, 'I am tired of the subject.'

'That won't do. Now, sit down.' She dragged him to a chair. 'Have the police done anything, Godfrey?' she asked him.

'No, nothing.'

'People say, don't they, Godfrey dear, that the three men who trapped you both are the Indians who came to Fritzinghall?'

'Some people say so, I believe, yes.'

'Do you?'

'My dear Rachel, I never saw their faces.' He tried to get up. She pushed him down. 'You never met Mr Luker before you met him at the bank?' He shook his head. 'You were questioned together by the police. Did the banker's receipt describe the object left at the bank?' He said the receipt wasn't mentioned in his presence. Rachel sighed. 'The newspapers are connecting what happened at Fritzinghall and what happened here. They say that the object in the bank is —' She stopped, her face suddenly white. Dear Mr Godfrey tried again to leave his chair. 'Stay where you are,' she ordered. 'They say it's the Moonstone, Godfrey. Don't they?'

To my surprise, a change came over my admirable friend. He lost his smoothness of manner. 'They *do* say so, yes! But Mr

Luker has repeatedly declared that he has never seen or heard of the Moonstone.' Rachel laughed. She looked at my friend pityingly. 'Did you know, Godfrey, that certain people are spreading rumours that you pawned the Moonstone to Luker?'

Suffering this terrible insult, his noble eyes filled with tears. He put out his hand to take hers. She jumped to her feet with a scream. 'Don't touch me!' she cried. She looked at her mother. 'This is all my fault! I sacrificed myself − I had a right to do that − but not to keep a secret that ruins an innocent man for life!'

'You exaggerate,' Mr Godfrey said. 'My reputation can't be ruined by rumours like that. All will be forgotten in a week.'

'I must stop it!' she cried out. 'I know who took the Moonstone, I know, I know −' She stamped on the ground in a peculiar temper. *I know that Godfrey is innocent!* She fell to her knees at her mother's feet. 'Oh, mamma, mamma, I must be mad, mustn't I?' Mr Godfrey attempted to calm her. Pulling herself together, she said, 'Godfrey, I've been so unfair to you. You're a better man than I believed. I'll try and repair the wrong I've done you.' She gave him her hand and − he actually kissed it!

'I will come, dearest,' he said, 'as long as you never mention this hateful subject again.' I was deeply shocked by our Christian Hero's behaviour. A thunderous knock at the door startled us all.

Rachel got up. 'They've come to take me to the flower show,' she said, teary-eyed. She kissed her mother. 'Mamma, before I go, this hasn't caused you too much anxiety, has it?'

'No, no, my dear, go with your friends now and enjoy yourself.'

She left the room. My heart bled for the poor misguided girl. Mr Godfrey gave us one of his beautiful smiles, held out a hand to his aunt, a hand to me. I closed my eyes, put his hand – in a moment of self-forgetfulness – to my lips and sat down. When I opened my eyes again he had gone.

But, alone with Lady Verinder, I was to hear worse. 'Drusilla,' she said. 'I have something to tell you, and a favour to ask you. My lawyer, Mr Bruff, is coming at five. I want you to witness the signing of my will. I have been seriously ill, Drusilla, for more than two years now, with heart disease, and the truth is I may live another year or die this afternoon.' She looked hard at me. 'Rachel, of course, must not be told.' How can I describe the sorrow and sympathy I felt, or the thrilling thankfulness that rushed through me? My dear aunt was totally unprepared to make the great change. 'Oh! Oh, how I can help you, aunt!' I said, forgetting myself. She gave me a puzzled, almost frightened look. 'Aunt,' I said, 'I have some books which you must read, books that can help you in this hour of need.' I had just time to hurry home, get the books and return for the signing of the will.

When I returned, the doctor was with Aunt Verinder. I joined Mr Bruff in the library. He was surprised to see me – we had met on similar occasions more than once. 'Have you come to stay here?' he said, eyeing my large bag full of books. 'My aunt has asked me to witness her will,' I said.

'I see,' he said. 'Very well – after all, you've no financial interest in it. So, tell me. Miss Clack, what's the latest news from the world of ladies' charity? How is your friend Godfrey Ablewhite? I've been hearing some salty stories about him.'

Understanding his meaning perfectly, I replied, 'I won't argue with a clever lawyer, Mr Bruff. I will simply say that in the eyes of a famous London police officer, there is not the slightest shadow of suspicion on anyone except Miss Verinder.'

'Do you mean,' he replied, 'that you agree with Cuff?'

'I mean nothing. I am a Christian, Mr Bruff, I judge no one.'

'I judge the Sergeant to have been completely wrong,' he replied. 'If he knew Rachel's character as I know it, he would never have suspected her. I admit she has her faults – she's wild, stubborn, secretive – but she's as honest and true as steel.'

I could not resist telling him the truth. 'In that case, permit me to inform you that when Mr Godfrey was here two hours ago Rachel declared that he was innocent.' I went on to describe the whole scene, everything that was said.

'You would have made a good lawyer, Miss Clack,' he said when I had finished. He began walking thoughtfully up and down. The new light I had thrown on the subject had obviously disturbed him. 'What a case!' I heard him say to himself. 'A complete mystery.'

'Excuse me,' I said. 'But may I remind you that Mr Franklin Blake was also in the house when the diamond disappeared? His debts are well known.' The old devil looked at me steadily with a hard and vicious smile. 'I manage Mr Franklin's legal affairs,' he said. 'And I can tell you that most of his lenders, knowing that his father is a very rich and very old man, are quite prepared to be patient. Besides, Lady Verinder has told me that her daughter is ready to marry Franklin Blake. She told her that she loved him. So, Miss Clack, why would he steal the jewel?'

'The human heart is unsearchable,' I said gently.

'No, no, Miss Clack,' he said, 'Miss Rachel's innocence is without doubt. So is Mr Ablewhite's. So is Mr Franklin's. All we know is that the Moonstone came to London, and that Mr Luker or his banker has it at the moment. It puzzles you, me, everybody.' A servant came in to say Aunt Verinder was ready to receive us.

Chapter 3   Placing the Books

My aunt's will was as short as her husband's. Her daughter would inherit everything. A handsome young servant, Samuel, was second witness. The signing took less than two minutes.

Afterwards, Mr Bruff looked at me, hoping perhaps that I might leave him alone with my aunt. He might as well have expected the Rock of Gibraltar to move. He said something under his breath and left. My aunt lay down on the sofa. 'I haven't forgotten you, dear,' she said. 'You're not mentioned in the will but I intend to give you something to remember me by.'

Here was a golden opportunity! I took a book out of my bag, *The Snake at Home*, by Miss Bellows. This fine Christian work shows how evil lies in wait for us in the most innocent actions of our daily lives. 'Read this book,' I said, 'and you will have given me all I could ever want.' My poor aunt glanced at the book and handed it back to me, looking more confused than ever.

'I'm afraid, Drusilla,' she said, 'that the doctor has advised me to read only amusing books.'

'Aunt,' I said patiently, 'let me leave it here.' She gave me an exhausted look, so I thought it might be wise to leave.

I crossed the hall and slipped into the library, where I noticed two of the 'amusing' books the doctor had recommended. I took out two of mine and put them on top of them. I went into the breakfast room, and put two more on the piano. I put a whole pile beside my aunt's sewing box, another by the fireplace.

As I folded my clothes that night I thought of the *true* riches I was giving to my wealthy aunt in the form of my good Christian books. I felt so light-hearted that I sang a song to Jesus! And forgot to pray for Rachel.

Next morning, as I was about to leave for Montagu Square, my landlady knocked. Samuel was standing beside her with a box, looking as fresh and blue-eyed as ever. I felt a Christian, motherly interest in the boy, so I invited him in. He put the box down, looking as though he wanted to run away, and said there was a letter inside. I delayed him with a few questions. Could I see my aunt if I called at Montagu Square? No, she had gone out for a drive with Miss Rachel and Mr Ablewhite. I also discovered that they were going to a concert together the following morning. I offered Samuel tea. He rushed out.

We had a meeting of the Young Mothers' Small Clothes Society that night. The next day there was a meeting of the British Ladies' Servants' Sunday Sweetheart Society. So obviously Mr Godfrey had no intention of being present at either. I was beginning to see our hero in a slightly different light.

Feverishly, I began opening the box. Was it the 'remembrance' my aunt had promised me? No, it was my twelve precious books. I admit I was a little disappointed but, as you know, the true Christian never gives up; so at two o'clock, there I was with my books again, knocking on Lady Verinder's door.

Miss Cap Ribbons said she had had a bad night and was resting on the sofa. I said I would wait in the library. I thought that Rachel and her pleasure-loving friends (Mr Godfrey included, alas!) were all at the concert. So, having placed books here and there, I decided to go upstairs and put some in the living-room. As I entered I heard a knock on the door downstairs, then heard Samuel say, 'Upstairs, if you please, sir.' I heard footsteps. Not wanting to be discovered upstairs on my own, I hurried into a small area on one side of the living-room and pulled the curtain. The man entered the living-room and began walking up and down, talking to himself. 'Do it today! You must do it today,' he kept saying. It was Godfrey Ablewhite.

Chapter 4   A Silent Listener

I was about to rush out and beg him, in the name of the Ladies' Committees, to explain himself, when I heard Rachel say, 'Why didn't you go into the library?' He laughed softly. 'Because I was told Miss Clack is in there.' She laughed. 'Clack, in the library!' she replied. 'You're right, Godfrey, we're much better here. Bring that chair nearer to me.' Carefully, I moved the curtain so I could see. 'Well?' she went on, 'What did you say to them?'

'Just what you said to say, dear. They were sad not to see you at the concert.' He brought his chair even closer and took her hand. Can words describe how saddened I was by this sight?

'Have you forgotten, Godfrey?' she said. 'We agreed to be cousins and nothing more.'

'My heart breaks that agreement, Rachel, every time I see you.'

'Then don't see me.'

'No! Am I mad, Rachel, to dream that one day your heart may soften to me?' He put his handkerchief to his eyes. Even *she* seemed to be moved.

'Are you really sure, Godfrey, that you are that fond of me?'

'You're my only interest in life. Would you believe that now my charitable duties seem like a nuisance to me? When I see a Ladies' Committee now I wish I was at the other end of the earth!'

'You've made your confession,' she said. 'Now I think the best thing you can do is leave. I'm not good enough for you, Godfrey. I hate myself, don't you understand?' She burst into tears. 'And I don't want your pity! Now go away, will you!' He did something completely unexpected. He knelt at her feet . . . and put both arms round her! 'Noble person,' he said.

Rachel was so surprised, or fascinated — I don't know which — that she made absolutely no effort to put his arms back where they should have been.

She was so surprised, or fascinated – I don't know which – that she made absolutely no effort to put his arms back where they should have been. 'Yes,' he repeated. 'You're such a noble person. Please let me be the one to take care of your poor wounded heart.'

'Godfrey,' she replied, drying her eyes. 'You must be mad!'

'I never spoke more seriously, my dearest. I don't ask for your love straight away. I'll be content simply with your affection and respect. Only Time can heal wounds as deep as yours.'

She looked at him, confusion clouding her face. 'Don't tempt me, Godfrey,' she said sadly. 'I'm unhappy and disturbed enough as it is. Don't tempt me to make things even worse!'

'One question, Rachel. Do you have anything against me?'

'I – I always liked you. I respect and admire you.'

'How many wives can say that, Rachel? How many respect and admire their husbands? Marry me, dearest! I value your respect and admiration more than the love of any other woman!'

'Slow down, Godfrey! You're putting something into my head which I never even thought of before.'

'I won't get up until you've said yes!'

She looked at him curiously. 'Do you feel as confidently as you speak, confident enough to give me time, not to hurry me?'

'My time shall be yours.'

'You won't ask me for more than I can give?'

'My Angel, all that I ask of you is your hand!'

'Take it then.'

With those words she accepted him! He pulled her nearer, until her face touched his, and she let him – I tried to close my eyes before it happened (I almost screamed in horror). When I opened them again he was sitting next to her. 'Shall I speak to your mother,' he asked, 'or shall you?'

She seemed to come to her senses. 'I don't want my mother to hear from either of us until she's better. Godfrey, go now. Come back this evening.' She got up and looked in my direction. 'Who closed those curtains?' She came towards me, was about to open the curtains when – my heart almost stopped – Samuel's voice shouted from downstairs. 'Miss Rachel! Where are you?' She ran to the door. 'Miss Rachel, my lady has fainted.'

Moments later I was alone. I went downstairs unseen and saw Mr Godfrey hurrying out to fetch the doctor. I found Rachel on her knees by the sofa. One look at my aunt was enough. She was dead. I was so shocked that I didn't remember until a few days later that she hadn't given me my little 'remembrance'.

Chapter 5   Brighton

Ten days after Lady Verinder's tragic death, the whole family knew about the secret marriage engagement. I didn't see Rachel until a month later. My aunt's will had named her brother-in-law, Godfrey Ablewhite's father, as Rachel's legal adviser.

Rachel wanted to move. The house in London reminded her of her poor mother, the house in Yorkshire reminded her of the terrible affair of the Moonstone. Old Mr Ablewhite suggested renting a house in Brighton. Mrs Ablewhite could come and stay there with her. He asked Mrs Ablewhite to make arrangements.

Aunt Ablewhite has never done a thing for herself in her life. She found the rented house in Brighton by staying at a hotel in London and asking her son to find it. She found the servants by inviting her niece to tea. 'Drusilla, dear, I want some servants. You're so clever. Please get them for me.' I went into the next room to make a list, and was surprised to see Rachel. She got up and took my hand. 'Drusilla,' she said, 'I've always been so rude to you. I do hope you'll forgive me.' Of course, like a good Christian, I accepted her apology. She invited me to come and stay with her in Brighton. There had been such a remarkable change in the poor child that I felt that I might at last be able to help her towards the only true happiness, the love of God. And the stay in Brighton would be a chance to begin the good work.

She suggested that I should go to Brighton first to prepare the house. I accepted. By Saturday afternoon I had found suitable servants and all was ready. The joy of being able to convert her to the Christian faith filled my mind with a heavenly peace. Having placed a few carefully chosen books in Rachel's rooms, I went downstairs to wait for them to arrive.

They arrived at six, not with Mr Godfrey, as I expected, but with the scheming old lawyer, Bruff. I had prepared a little heaven for my Rachel and here was a snake already! Rachel went over to the window and stared at the sea. 'Tired, love?' I enquired.

'No,' she replied. 'Just a little sad – remembering happy days that can never come again. I've often seen the sea in Yorkshire with that light on it.'

Bruff stayed the evening. I was sure he had a reason for accompanying them to Brighton. When he finally left for his hotel he invited himself to lunch the next day.

The next morning I took Rachel to church. At lunch, she refused to eat, saying she had a headache. The lawyer jumped at his chance. 'A walk is a good cure for a headache,' he said. 'I'll accompany you.' She accepted his offer enthusiastically.

'It's past two,' I remarked gently. 'Afternoon church is at three.' But a minute later they had left the house.

They had got back when I returned from church. One look

told me the lawyer had said what he wanted to say. I had never seen Rachel so silent and thoughtful. Bruff got up to leave. He had (or pretended he had) to be in London the next day. 'Are you sure of your decision?' he said. 'Quite sure,' she said. When he had left she went to her room and did not come down to dinner.

When I took up her cup of tea the next morning, I asked her whether she had had time to look at any of my books. Yes, she said, and they had not interested her. 'I was wondering, my love,' I said, 'whether Mr Bruff might have told you some bad news?' Her dark eyes flashed at me. 'No, not at all,' she said. 'It was most interesting news.' She looked out at the sea. 'I suppose,' I said with gentle interest, 'that it was news about Mr Godfrey?' She thought a moment then said these remarkable words: *'I shall never marry Godfrey Ablewhite.'*

'What can you possibly mean?' I exclaimed. 'The marriage is considered by everyone to be a settled thing!' She looked at me very seriously. 'Wait until Godfrey Ablewhite comes here today,' she said, 'and you will see. Now, please, Drusilla, I'm going to have a bath.' It was the best way of making me leave the room.

After breakfast she wandered aimlessly from room to room, then suddenly sat down at the piano and began hammering out shameful tunes from the most un-Christian shows. I was forced to leave the house. Returning, I entered the dining-room and found myself face to face with Godfrey Ablewhite. He made no attempt to leave. On the contrary, he came warmly forward to greet me. 'Dear Miss Clack, I've been waiting to see you!' He knew my friends must have kept me informed of his shameful neglect of our charities. Perhaps he wanted to explain his behaviour.

'Have you seen Rachel yet?' I asked. He sighed gently, and took me by the hand. I'm sure I wouldn't have let him if he hadn't given me this astonishing reply:

'Yes,' he said perfectly calmly, 'and we talked about our engagement. She has decided to leave me free to make a happier choice elsewhere. And I have agreed.' I stood staring at him, my hand in his. He led me to a chair. 'Suppose we sit down,' he said sweetly. The man has such a way with ladies I felt completely helpless. I remember he was very affectionate.

'I have lost a beautiful girl, an excellent social position, and a large income,' he began. 'I have agreed to it without a struggle, and curiously I don't care. Now, when I think about it, I don't even know why I proposed marriage to her. The result, however, is that I have neglected my dear Ladies. I feel like a child who doesn't know why he's been naughty.' I remember he became even more affectionate (he even put his arm round my waist).

'Dear friend,' he went on, 'the idea of marrying Rachel seems to me now like a strange dream. My true happiness is with my dear Ladies, in doing my modest Christian work. I don't need an income! Or a social position! Or Miss Verinder! A month ago I was pressing her to my chest. Today she told me she loves another man and that marrying me was an attempt to forget him. Can you explain my behaviour, my dear friend? I certainly can't.'

I could. The pure Christian side of him had finally rejected the idea of marriage to Rachel. I told him this in a few sisterly words. His joy was beautiful. He compared himself to a man coming out of darkness into light. Our brother had returned among us! I let him do what he liked with his hands. I felt my eyes closing in self-forgetfulness . . . Then the dinner bell rang. I jumped up.

'I must rush to the station,' he exclaimed. I asked him why he was in such a hurry. 'I must tell my father about this – his heart was set on our marriage.' He hurried out. I went in to lunch, naturally curious to see how all this had affected Miss Rachel. She was silent, distant, yet seemed to be relieved. I had the impression she felt free again to think about the man she loved.

I was sure old Mr Ablewhite would arrive that night – considering the importance his greed had attached to his son's marriage to Rachel. He arrived the next day, followed soon afterwards by Mr Bruff. 'Well, this is a surprise, Mr Bruff,' he said. 'When I left you yesterday I hardly expected to see you here today.'

'After our conversation,' Bruff replied, 'I thought perhaps I might be of some use.' He seated himself by Rachel. Mr Ablewhite stayed purposefully in the middle of the room. 'Rachel, my dear,' he said most affectionately. 'I have heard some very extraordinary news. Please, would you come into the sitting-room with me?'

'Whatever you want to say to me can be said here in the presence of my –' (she glanced at Mr Bruff) '– of my mother's old and trusted friend.'

'Very well, my dear,' Mr Ablewhite said patiently. He took a chair, smiling sympathetically at her. 'It's obvious you two have had a lovers' quarrel.'

'Let us understand each other, Mr Ablewhite,' she said. 'No quarrel took place between your son and me. If he told you I suggested breaking our engagement, and that he agreed – he told you the truth.'

Mr Ablewhite went slightly red but replied sweetly. 'Come, come, my dear! Don't get angry. And don't be hard on poor Godfrey. He means well.'

'Mr Ablewhite, we have agreed to remain cousins. Is that clear?'

He went a shade redder. 'Must I understand then that your engagement is broken?'

'That is what you must understand, Mr Ablewhite. And that is all I have to say.' She turned and stared out at the sea.

Getting up, Mr Ablewhite pushed his chair back so violently it fell over. 'If my son doesn't feel insulted, I do!' he announced.

Rachel looked at him, surprised. 'Insult?' she said.

Mr Ablewhite was now purple. 'Yes, insult!' he repeated. 'I wasn't considered good enough for your mother's sister and now my son isn't good enough for you!'

A few wise words will help them, I thought to myself, and I got up. 'As an affectionate well-wisher,' I said, holding up one of my books, 'I am sure that these Christian words of love may –' Mr Ablewhite knocked the book out of my hand. 'Shut up!' he shouted, and turned to Rachel again. 'It is my duty to inform you, young woman, that if my son isn't good enough for you then I certainly can't be good enough to remain your legal adviser.' He smiled bitterly, bowed and marched out of the room.

'You idiot!' said Aunt Ablewhite, turning on me. 'You're the one who annoyed him! I hope I never see you and your stupid books again.' She went over to Rachel and kissed her. 'I beg my husband's pardon, my dear. Please, is there anything I can do?'

'Answering for Miss Verinder,' said Bruff, 'could I ask you to leave the room for ten minutes?' She left without a word. He looked hard at me, expecting me to follow, but soon gave up. 'My dear Rachel.' he said, 'would you like to come to stay with us in Hampstead – until we've decided what to do next?' She nodded, before I could even say a word.

'Stop!' I said. 'Mr Bruff! You're not her relative! I am. I invite her.' Rachel looked at me with cruel astonishment. Bruff said nothing. 'Rachel, dearest Rachel, come and share my modest home with me!'

'You're very kind, Drusilla,' she said. 'But I have accepted Mr Bruff's invitation.'

'Oh Rachel!' I cried, 'please don't say that! Please don't go! I dream of making a Christian out of you – like I was trying to do with your poor dear mother.' I tried to take her in my arms but she jumped back, looking at me almost in horror. 'Enough of your insults!' she cried. 'My mother was the most Christian person I have ever known.' She turned to the lawyer. 'It disgusts me to breathe the same air as her. Now, Mr Bruff, I must prepare to leave.' I was left there, alone, abandoned, hated by them all.

SECOND NARRATIVE

by Mathew Bruff, lawyer

Chapter 1   Money-Lending

I can throw some light on certain points which have remained in the dark. My narrative begins shortly after Lady Verinder's death, when I heard of Miss Verinder's proposed marriage.

I was terribly disappointed when I heard that she was to marry a man I had always believed to be a smooth-tongued flatterer. I was certain of his financial motives and felt it was my duty to warn Miss Rachel, but I did not want to worry her so soon after her mother's death. On the other hand, if I remained silent she would go ahead with a marriage that would make her unhappy for life.

I called at the hotel in London where Mrs Ablewhite and Miss Rachel were staying. They were going to Brighton the next day. Unexpectedly, Mr Godfrey could not accompany them, so I offered to. I was able to talk to Miss Rachel the next day. I recommended that she should tell Ablewhite in private that she had proof of his financial motives, and that therefore the marriage was out of the question. I told her to tell him that if he tried to oppose her, she would make her knowledge public.

After I returned that evening, Ablewhite's father came to my office. He told me that his son had been dismissed by Miss Rachel – *and had accepted it.* This confirmed my theory: that Godfrey needed a large sum of money and needed it *quickly.* Why else would he give up so easily a lifetime of luxury? His father wanted to know whether I had an explanation for Miss Verinder's extraordinary behaviour. Obviously, as her lawyer, I didn't have one. I was sure that Miss Verinder might find him difficult to cope with when he visited the next day. I thought it better if I was with her. The meeting has been described by Miss Clack and resulted in Miss Rachel coming to stay with my wife and me.

A week after the end of her stay with us, my secretary informed me that a gentleman wanted to see me. There was a foreign name on the man's card; below it, was handwritten: 'Recommended by Septimus Luker.' He was extremely polite, well-mannered, and very smartly dressed in European clothes. The moment he entered my office I knew he was one of the three Indians. I felt uneasy – knowing he would have murdered me if he thought I had the Moonstone. I asked what his business was.

He unfolded a gold cloth and showed me a tiny box, beautifully decorated with jewels. 'I have come, sir,' he said, 'to ask you to lend me some money. I can leave this as a guarantee.'

'Luker recommended me?' I asked. He nodded. 'Yet he knows I'm a lawyer, not a money-lender like him. He refused you?' He nodded. 'And so do I,' I said. He wrapped up the box and got up. 'Supposing, sir,' he said, 'that you could have lent me money, how long would you have given me to pay it back?'

'A year,' I replied.

'Is that the usual time in this country?' he asked. When I said it was, he smiled contentedly and bowed. I felt sure for some reason, as I watched him leave, that pawning the box was just an excuse to lead up to that very last question.

Shortly afterwards, Luker came to see me. The substance of what that slippery old crook had to say is this:

The Indian had visited him the day before, dressed in the same way. Luker recognized him as one of the Indians who had been begging at his house. Knowing that he must also be one of the men who had robbed him of his banker's receipt, Luker was terrified. The man showed him the box and asked for a loan. Luker refused, saying the best person to ask was a respectable lawyer. He recommended me. I asked him what the Indian had said before leaving. He had asked the same question, and got the same answer. A year.

Chapter 2   Next June

By an extraordinary coincidence I met Mr Murthwaite at a dinner that evening. Knowing he was a friend of Lady Verinder's, I brought up the subject of the Moonstone. 'Have you heard from the Indians lately?' he asked immediately. I described what had happened to Luker and myself, mentioning the Indian's question about the standard length of time for repaying a loan.

'Can't you see his motive, Mr Bruff?' he said. I said I couldn't. 'Which was the event that gave the Indians their first chance of taking the diamond?' he asked me. 'When Colonel Herncastle died,' I replied. 'Until then the stone was safe in the bank.'

'Yes,' he said. 'And you, as a lawyer, know that anyone can obtain a copy of a will from the Law Office. The copy of the Colonel's will informed them that he left the stone to Miss Verinder, and that Mr Blake or someone of his choice had to give it to her on her birthday. Their one difficulty was to decide whether to attempt to get hold of the diamond when it was removed from the bank, or later, in Yorkshire. They chose the

66

second, safest way – but were undoubtedly unaware, when they first visited Lady Verinder's house, that Franklin Blake had already put the stone in the bank in Fritzinghall. So they decided to wait until Miss Verinder's birthday; and were rewarded for their patience by the sight of the jewel on Miss Verinder's dress! However, the extraordinary disappearance of the Moonstone that night completely defeated their careful plan; and the next day they sat in jail, powerless to do anything. Their next chance came while they were still locked up. I'll explain. A day or two before they were set free the governor of the prison came to see me with a letter, addressed to the Indians at their hotel in Fritzinghall. It was written in Hindustani. I translated it: "Brothers, in the name of the Prince of the Night, turn your faces south and come to me in the street of many noises which leads to the muddy river. My own eyes have seen it." The day they were set free they took the first train to London. What was the next we heard of them?'

'They were annoying Luker, begging at his house,' I said.

'Somebody took the Moonstone to London and tried to pawn it, otherwise it would never have been in his possession. Have the police not found out who?' I shook my head. 'I see,' he said. 'At any rate, thanks to Luker's cleverness, the Indians lost their next chance of getting hold of the diamond. The Moonstone was once more out of their reach, in the bank, until –'

'Until next June,' I said. 'It was at the end of last June.'

'Exactly. They've been defeated twice. I don't believe they will let it happen a third time.' Those were his last words on the subject. That night I made a note in my diary about June next year. I close my narrative with what it said: *June 1849 – expect news of Indians towards end of month.*

Contributed by Franklin Blake

Chapter 1   Franklin's Return

In the spring of 1849, while I was travelling in Central Asia, I sent a servant to fetch my letters and money from the nearest British embassy. He returned with a letter from Mr Bruff. He advised me to return home immediately. My father had died.

Although I had put half the world between me and Rachel I had failed to forget her. The nearer I got to England, and to the possibility of seeing her, the more I felt her hold on my heart tightening again. She was the first person I asked after when Mr Bruff met me at the station. He told me she was living with a sister of the late Sir John Verinder, in Portland Place, London. Half an hour later I was on my way there.

The servant who answered the door wasn't sure whether Miss Verinder was at home or not. I sent him upstairs with my card. He came down again and informed me that she was out. I said I would call again at 6 p.m. That evening I was told again that she was not at home. It was clear. She did not wish to see me.

My servant took a letter to her the next day, with instructions to wait for an answer. There was none.

That afternoon, after Mr Bruff had told me of the events since my departure, I felt even more determined to find out the secret of her silence towards her mother, and of her cruel behaviour towards me. I decided to take the next train to Yorkshire. If it was humanly possible, I would find the thief who took the Moonstone!

There I was, standing on the familiar terrace, just before sunset that evening. I walked round to the back of the peaceful old house and saw dear old Betteredge in his chair with his pipe. 'Mr

Franklin!' he exclaimed and struggled to his feet. He shook his head regretfully. 'You still owe me that halfpenny.'

He invited me inside. I had to refuse – the house was Rachel's now. He was understandably disappointed. 'I had hoped things might have smoothed themselves over between you two,' he said. I took him by the arm. 'It's a lovely evening,' I said. 'I'll walk to Fritzinghall and stay at the hotel.'

'What brings you here, sir?' he asked. 'The Moonstone,' I replied. He looked at me curiously, appearing to wonder whether this was a joke. 'I intend to find out who took it,' I said. He became very serious. 'Now you listen to me,' he said. 'You leave that evil diamond alone! Don't waste your time on it. How can you hope to succeed where the great Cuff failed?'

I told him my mind was made up. I knew last year that the diamond was at the bottom of Rachel's dramatic change in attitude towards me, I knew it still was.

'But don't you feel afraid, sir,' he enquired, 'about what you might possibly find out about Miss Rachel – concerning her secret?'

'I'm as certain of her as you are,' I said. 'Knowing her secret won't change my love for her.' Reassured; he said, 'Then I can tell you, sir, that you may not have far to look.' I stared at him in the gathering darkness. 'Our poor Rosanna left a letter behind her, addressed to *you*. Limping Lucy has it, sir. She wouldn't give it to anyone except you. It was too late – you'd already left England. We'll go to the fishing village, sir, first thing tomorrow!'

Chapter 2   Instructions

I left the hotel before breakfast the next morning. Betteredge was waiting for me at the house, excitement showing through his characteristic calm.

When we arrived at the cottage, Mrs Yolland was in the kitchen with a thin, wild-looking girl with beautiful hair. She looked at me as if I was an object of both horror and fascination and limped upstairs. Mrs Yolland apologized for her daughter's odd behaviour. I heard 'thump, thump,' across the room above us, 'thump, thump,' downstairs again. And there she was with the letter in her hand. She made a sign for me to come with her. I followed her down to the beach, behind some fishing boats. 'I want to look at you,' she said. She fixed her eyes mercilessly on me. 'No, I can't see what she saw in him. Oh my poor lost darling! What could she see in this man?' She pushed the envelope into my hand. 'Take it!' she said bitterly and limped away.

The envelope contained a letter and a note. I read the letter first:

Sir, if you want to know the meaning of my behaviour towards you, follow the instructions in the note. You must do this alone.

The instructions gave me precise directions how to find a particular rock at the Shivering Sand, how to find a particular part of that rock (uncovered only at low tide), to feel around in the sea plants below it until I felt a chain, and to pull on that chain.

I heard Betteredge behind me. 'I can't stand it any longer, sir. For God's sake, what does it say?' I handed him the note. 'Cuff said it!' he cried, reading it. He looked at the sea. 'The tide is going down. It will turn in an hour.'

Following the instructions, we found the place twenty minutes before the turn of the tide. Betteredge turned to leave. 'Why are you leaving?' I asked. He reminded me of Rosanna's wish that I make the discovery alone. 'I'll wait up the beach,' he said.

I waited, watching, as the morning sun poured beauty on

I waited, watching, as the morning sun poured beauty on everything around me.

everything around me. The sweetness of the air made the simple act of living and breathing a luxury. The wet quicksand shone like gold. At last, the turn of the tide came. I saw the quicksand begin to move, an awful tremble creeping across its surface. I climbed down the slippery rock until my face was almost touching the quicksand. For an instant a terrible fear gripped me. I thought she might rise up out of it and pull me in. I reached down among the plants underwater – and touched the chain. I pulled, and up out of the quicksand it came: a metal case.

I opened it and pulled out a white nightgown. There was also a letter. I spread out the nightgown, saw the smear of paint on it. Sergeant Cuff's words returned to me: 'Find the dress with the stain, find out who it belongs to, and you haven't far to look for the hand that took the diamond.' I looked at the label on the nightgown and read the name. F R A N K L I N B L A K E .

Chapter 3   Rosanna's Letter

The shock of it stopped all thinking and feeling. The next thing I remember is walking back with Betteredge, and then his little sitting-room. In the state I was in, the old man was an enormous comfort to me. 'I have absolutely no knowledge of taking the diamond,' I told him. 'The very idea of my taking it is ridiculous! But here are the facts: my nightgown, the paint on it!'

'I smell something suspicious, sir,' said Betteredge, pouring me another whisky. 'Was there anything else in the case?' I was instantly reminded of the letter. I opened it. There were many pages, signed at the end by Rosanna Spearman.

'Wait,' I said. 'How do we know she didn't steal the diamond? She may have smeared the nightgown deliberately.' Betteredge put his hand on my arm. 'In justice to the girl's memory, sir, see what the letter says.' This is what it said:

Sir, I shall be dead when you read this, but I have a confession to make. I love you.

Why did I hide your nightgown with the paint on it? Why did I say nothing to you about it? Because I loved you. Do you remember when you met us on the beach that morning? You came to me, like a lover in a dream. From that moment on I loved you more and more each minute, completely forgetting who I was – only a servant, not a lady. I believe I found out you were in love with Miss Rachel before you knew it yourself. Would you have loved her if she was a servant?

The morning the diamond disappeared, after Seegrave pointed out the smear on the door and said someone's dress had done it, he sent us all back to our work. After I had left Miss Rachel's room, Penelope saw me looking to see if I had any paint on my dress and told me not to bother. The paint had been dry for hours, she said. She had heard Mr Franklin tell Miss Rachel that it would take twelve hours to dry. They had finished the door at 3 p.m. Therefore it had dried around three that morning.

It was my job, sir, to clean your room. It was the happiest hour of the day for me. I used to kiss your pillow – I beg your pardon, I'm forgetting myself. Well, that morning, I saw the smear of paint on your nightgown. It was proof you had been in Miss Rachel's sitting-room between midnight and three that morning! I was so shocked I ran to my room with it. At the time I never even thought you might have taken the diamond. I decided to keep the nightgown and wait and watch, to see what use I might make of it. But how could I keep it without risking being found out? The only way was to make another one exactly the same.

I had just finished your room when I was called to be questioned by Seegrave. Next, all the servants' wardrobes were searched. Later, after Penelope was questioned a second time, she came back to the kitchen

73

boiling with anger. According to her, Seegrave suspected her because she was the last person in Miss Rachel's sitting-room that night. I knew you had been there later. My head began to spin when I realized: YOU were the thief! Deliberately, you had been the most active the next day, organizing the search, fetching the police just to deceive us.

I believed you were guilty because I wanted you to be guilty. It gave me power over you, power to destroy you in Rachel's eyes. I had the nightgown that was the only proof against you. But you would miss it. I needed cloth to make the new one so, after lunch, I pretended to feel ill. Sergeant Cuff, I know, discovered later that I was not in my room all that afternoon. But others already suspected me. That night, as I was working in secret, I heard two servants whispering outside my door.

There was a knock on the door. 'Come in!' Betteredge shouted. One of the strangest looking men I have ever seen entered. Judging by his figure and movements, he was still young, but his face told another story: he might have been older than Betteredge. His skin was coffee-coloured, his nose like those of the ancient peoples of the East. Dark, dreamy eyes, hollow fleshless cheeks added to his odd appearance. But it was his hair which was the most remarkable. Originally dark and curly, it had gone white in the most extraordinary manner: in stripes here and there, like spilt paint. Seeing me staring stupidly at him, he said, 'I beg your pardon,' and handed a piece of paper to Betteredge. His eyes rested on me again, and he left the room as quietly as he had entered.

'Who was that?' I asked.

'Ezra Jennings, Dr Candy's assistant,' replied Betteredge. 'Poor Dr Candy never recovered from his illness, I'm afraid. He lost his memory. Jennings takes care of the few patients he has left – poor people mostly.'

'You don't seem to like him,' I remarked.

'Nobody does, sir – because of his appearance, I suppose, and the colour of his skin. He's a quiet man, keeps himself to himself. He came with the list of the sick. Miss Rachel has carried on her mother's tradition of taking wine to the poor people who are sick.'

I began reading again:

I knew Sergeant Cuff would want to examine our clothes. There was nowhere in my room where I could hide the nightgown, so I undressed and put it on under my dress. I was asked to take the washing book to Sergeant Cuff. He and I had already met more than once, but he treated me as if I was a stranger. I knew this was a bad sign. Afterwards, as it was time for your return from taking Mr Ablewhite to the station, I went to your favourite walk near the rose garden. It was the last chance, perhaps, that I might have to speak to you. You never appeared, and worse – Sergeant Cuff saw me hiding there.

Why didn't I go and see you later? Why didn't I go and say, 'I have something to say to you, Mr Franklin. You must listen!' I could have done – I had such power over you! I had heard Mr Betteredge talk about your debts. You were obviously going to pawn the diamond. I could have told you of a man in London who would have taken the jewel. Why didn't I speak to you? When I was a thief I had taken much greater risks. What was I afraid of? You, Mr Franklin. In my dreams I loved you with all my heart. Before your face . . . I was afraid of you.

Everyone was questioned by Sergeant Cuff. My bitterest enemies, the cook and Lady Verinder's maid, went in before me. He was very careful to hide it but I knew that after speaking to them he suspected me of making a new nightgown secretly – and therefore of being involved in the disappearance of the diamond. The great Cuff was miles from the truth! You were safe as long as the nightgown was safe.

If I had been less fond of you I would have destroyed it. But I couldn't − it was the only thing that could prove to you that I had saved you. It was your debt to me.

After the interview I said I was feeling ill and needed some fresh air. I went straight to the Yollands' house. Here I am now, writing. When I have finished I shall go to the Shivering Sand, hide the nightgown and then − what then? I will leave this cruel world that has refused me the happiness it gives so easily to others. Don't blame yourself for this, sir, but try − please try − to remember me kindly. If you do, I believe my ghost will tremble with joy.

I love you, sir, Rosanna Spearman.

Chapter 4   Return to London

I decided to go back to London that day, present the facts to Mr Bruff, and obtain an interview (no matter how) with Rachel.

'Betteredge,' I asked as we were walking to the station, 'have you ever known me to walk in my sleep?' He nodded. 'I see your meaning, sir,' he replied. 'And the answer is no. But if we are to believe the nightgown, then you went to the room that night − without knowing it − and you took the diamond − without knowing it. How that is possible I don't know, but if it is, how can the diamond have found its way to London − without you knowing it?' I said nothing. I was so upset I couldn't think straight.

We reached the station a few minutes early. I noticed Ezra Jennings by the book stall. He took off his hat to me.

In London I went straight to Mr Bruff's house in Hampstead. He examined the nightgown and read Rosanna Spearman's letter. 'Mr Franklin,' he said, 'this is a very serious matter − for Miss Rachel as much as for you. Her extraordinary behaviour is no mystery now. She believes you took the diamond. She must be persuaded or forced to tell us why she thinks this. As a lawyer, I can tell you that the evidence against you falls down, firstly, on one important point. There must be proof that *you* wore that nightgown when it was smeared. There is also Miss Spearman's letter. It shows that she was clever. If Rachel suspected you simply on the proof of the nightgown then I'm sure it was Rosanna who showed it to her. It was her opportunity to destroy the love between you and Miss Rachel. Search your memory. While you were staying at the house, did anything happen to make Rachel doubt your honesty?'

I immediately remembered the Frenchman's visit. I had foolishly accepted a loan in Paris. My aunt had paid him, but 'she had been shocked by my irresponsibility. Rachel heard about it and said some severe things to me. 'I must speak to Rachel myself,' I said. 'I know that somewhere in her heart she still has some affection for me. The question is how – how to see her?' The lawyer gave this some thought. 'I'll invite her here the day after tomorrow,' he said. 'Expect a call from me that morning.'

The next day was the longest in my life. The day after, Bruff came early and gave me a key. 'She's coming to lunch and will stay the afternoon. This is the key to the garden gate. At three, let yourself in. The living-room door will be open. Go in and open the door into the music room. You'll find her there alone.'

Later that morning I received a letter from Betteredge. Jennings had stopped him at the station and asked who I was. Later, he had mentioned me to Dr Candy. The doctor had said he particularly wanted to see me, whenever I returned to Fritzinghall. He asked Betteredge to let me know this.

The clock of Hampstead church struck three as I stepped into the garden. The birds were my only witnesses. I crossed the empty living-room to the music room door. She was playing the piano. The tune brought back a wave of memories. I had to wait and pull myself together. Finally, I opened the door.

Chapter 5   Witness

She got up, and we faced each other in silence. 'Rachel!' I said gently. She advanced, as though against her own wishes, her cheeks a warm dusky colour. I forgot everything, saw only the woman I loved walking towards me. I took her in my arms, covered her face with kisses. There was a moment when I thought my kisses were returned but then suddenly she let out a little cry, like a cry of horror, and pushed me away from her. I saw merciless anger in her eyes, total contempt on her lips. 'You miserable heartless coward!' she said. 'After what you've done, you play on my weakness, trick me into letting you kiss me!'

'You say "what you've done". What have I done?'

'What have you done?' she cried. 'You dare ask me that! I kept your crime a secret – and suffered the consequences. You were once a gentleman, dear to my mother, dear to me –' She dropped into a chair and buried her face in her hands.

'Rachel,' I said, 'I came here to tell you something very important. Will you at least just listen to what I have to say?' She neither moved nor answered.

I told her of my discovery at the Shivering Sand. She never said a word, never even looked at me. 'I have a question to ask you,' I said. 'Did she show you the nightgown? Yes or no?'

She jumped to her feet, looked at me searchingly, as though trying to read something in my eyes. 'Are you mad?' she said.

I simply replied, 'Rachel, will you answer my question, please?'

Her lips curled into a bitter smile. 'They say your father's death has made you a rich man. Have you come here to repay me for the loss of my diamond?'

I could control myself no longer. 'You've done me wrong!' I cried. 'You suspect me of stealing your diamond. I have a right to know why!'

'Suspect you!' she exclaimed. *'I saw you take it with my own eyes!'*

I stood there speechless.

'Why did you come here?' she asked contemptuously. I advanced towards her, hardly conscious of what I was doing. The only words I could find were, 'Rachel, you once loved me.' I took her hand. She looked away, her hand trembling in mine. 'Let go of me!' she said faintly.

I led her gently to the sofa and sat her down beside me. 'Rachel,' I said, 'I can't possibly explain what I'm going to say. Yet it is the truth. You say you saw me take the diamond with your own eyes. What I say is this: I now realize – for the first time – that I took it. Do you still doubt my sincerity?'

'Let go of me,' she repeated weakly, but her head sank to my shoulder, her hand unconsciously closed around mine. 'Tell me everything that happened,' I said, 'from when we said goodnight to when you saw me take the diamond.' She lifted her head, made an effort to release her hand. 'Why go back to it?' she said.

'I'll tell you why,' I replied. 'Because we're the victims of some horrible trick.' Tears fell slowly over her cheeks. 'Oh!' she whispered, 'Oh, how I've tried to persuade myself that.' I held her closer. 'You tried alone, without me to help you.' My words seemed to awaken hope in her. 'What happened after we left each other that night? Did you go straight to bed?' She nodded.

'About twelve o'clock, but I couldn't sleep – I was thinking of you.' Her answer almost brought tears to my eyes. 'I got up at about one o'clock,' she continued, 'and lit a candle. I was about to go into my sitting-room to get a book. I had just opened the door – but hadn't gone in – when I saw a light under the other door and heard footsteps approaching along the corridor. I thought it was my mother, coming to try and persuade me to let her take care of the diamond. I blew out the candle so she would think I was in bed. The moment I blew it out the door opened and I saw –'

'You saw?'

'You. In your nightgown, a candle in your hand.'

'Were my eyes open?'

'Yes. They were very bright. You came into the middle of the room, looking around you, as though afraid of being found out. I was so terrified I couldn't speak or even move to shut the door. You could easily have seen me, but you didn't. I'm sure you never saw me.' I asked her how she was sure. 'If you'd seen me you wouldn't have taken the diamond. You went straight to the cabinet and opened drawers until you found it. I saw the stone shining in your hand as you took it out. You stood there for what seemed like ages, thinking, seemingly uneasy about something. Then you left. You went straight out, leaving the door open. I stood there in the dark listening to your steps dying away.'

I got up and walked up and down. 'So?' she said. 'What do you have to say now?' She waited pitilessly for my reply. I had none, only the terrible, shameful helplessness of my situation. I suddenly felt the horror, the disappointment she must have felt. I turned and opened the door to leave. She jumped up, closed the door. 'No!' she said, 'Not yet.' She spoke without looking at me. 'I won't tell you what I felt, Franklin. I'll simply tell you what I did. I decided to tell no one. I was prepared to believe anything – no matter what! – rather than believe you were a thief. I raised

You went straight to the cabinet and opened drawers until you found it. I saw the stone shining in your hand as you took it out.

the alarm the next morning. And what was the first news I heard afterwards? I heard that YOU had called the police! You were working harder than anyone to recover the jewel that you already had! But even then – even then something wouldn't let me give up my faith in you. I went down to the terrace and forced myself to speak to you – have you forgotten what I said?' I could have answered, but for what purpose? 'I know what I said,' she went on. 'I gave you several opportunities – didn't I? – to tell me the truth. I let you know in the clearest possible way – without actually saying it – that I knew you had stolen it. All you did was look at me with your false face of innocence – just as you are now, as if a few words could end a little misunderstanding! I saw you steal it! I saw you pretend to help the police! You pawned it in London and ran away abroad the next morning. And now you come here and tell me I have wronged you!'

I brushed past her and opened the door. She caught my arm. 'Let me go,' I said. But she wouldn't. 'Why did you come here?' she said. 'Why? Are you afraid I might make the truth known – now that you're a rich man? You can marry anyone you want now, can't you?' She gave me a terrible look and suddenly let go of me. 'Yet even now I can't tear you out of my heart! Oh, God! I hate myself even more than I hate you.'

I broke free and left her. 'Franklin!' she cried after me. 'I forgive you! Oh, Franklin, Franklin, shall we never meet again? Say you forgive *me*!' I turned, seeing her only dimly through my tears, before I left the garden.

Chapter 6   Investigating

Late that evening Mr Bruff visited me, not at all his usual confident self. 'You know the truth at last,' he said. 'However, the price you – both of you – paid was too much. She's young.

She will get over this, with time. Promise me, Mr Franklin, that you won't try and see her again, will you?'

'You have my word.'

'Now, in my opinion, it would be better to consider the inexplicable events which Miss Rachel described as – dead and buried.' He saw my total confusion. 'We're wasting our time in the past, Mr Franklin. We must look to the future. What do we know? We know it was pawned to Mr Luker. Do we know who by? No. Where is it now? In Luker's bank. And there is every chance that the person who pawned it may want to get it back. It is already June – almost a year since it was put in the bank. So I suggest watching the bank. However, if Murthwaite is right, then the Indians will be watching it too. Whatever happens, we must find out *who* pawned the diamond. Only the discovery of the thief can restore you to your rightful place in Miss Rachel's heart. It means waiting about a fortnight at the most.'

'A lifetime,' I said. 'My existence is a horrible dream. I must do something now! I had thought of contacting Sergeant Cuff...'

'Useless. He has retired from the police.' I told him I knew where to find him. 'All right, do what you want,' said Bruff, picking up his hat. 'Yes, it's worth a try. As for me, I'll take care of the bank.' We parted.

Next morning, as I walked up the garden path of a little cottage in Dorking, I saw Cuff's favourite flower everywhere around me. Far from the crimes of the great city, he was living out his last years here. His wife told me he was in Ireland on rose business. For how long? She didn't know. I gave her my card and asked whether he could contact me as soon as he returned.

For most of that night I sat smoking, building up wild hopeless theories and knocking them down again. The next morning, pure chance rescued me from my confusion. I put on the coat I was wearing the day I visited Rachel and found Betteredge's letter in a pocket. I read it again. Dr Candy had said he wanted to say something very important to me. I wondered what it could be – something about the birthday evening, perhaps? Instinct told me to go to Yorkshire that day. The next train left three hours later. As I sat wondering how to kill the time, my thoughts kept wandering back to the birthday dinner. I tried to remember all the guests. Most of them were from Fritzinghall, except Godfrey, Mr Murthwaite and Miss Clack. I decided to pay Godfrey a visit.

I drove to his club, where I met a friend in the hall, a friend of Godfrey's also. He told me that shortly after Rachel broke off their engagement, he had made an offer of marriage to another very rich young lady – who accepted, but a few days later the engagement was suddenly broken off. Soon afterwards, Godfrey was extremely generously remembered in the will of a very rich old lady, a member of the Young Mothers' Etc., Etc. Society. She had also been a friend of Miss Clack but had only left her a ring.

Five thousand pounds richer, Godfrey felt the need for a rest from his charitable activities. He had left London for Europe the previous day and was expected to be gone at least three months.

I arrived too late in Fritzinghall to see Betteredge. The next morning I sent a messenger to ask him to come to my hotel. I decided to visit Dr Candy before he came.

When I saw the once lively little doctor, I could hardly recognize him. His eyes were dim, his face thin and grey. The man was a wreck. 'Yes, I have often thought of you, Mr Blake,' the poor man said, then forgot what he wanted to say next.

'You remember the mysterious loss of the Indian diamond,' I said. 'I'm trying to find it. I need to find out everything I can about what happened at the birthday party. There may be a clue. Do you remember anything out of the ordinary?' The doctor picked restlessly at his fingers, his dull eyes fixed emptily on me. The man had no idea what I was talking about. 'You sent a message to Gabriel Betteredge, saying you wanted to see me.' I said.

'Yes, yes . . . ,' he said. 'That's it! I sent you a message!' He tried to remember why.

I tried to help. 'It's been nearly a year now since the dinner at Lady Verinder's. It was the last time we saw each other.'

'Ah, the dinner, the dinner!' he said. 'Yes, I've something to say to you about that.' He looked at me with a painful expression of enquiry, desperately trying to remember. 'Yes, it was a most pleasant dinner,' he said.

By this time I had been with him nearly an hour. Not wanting to tire him, I rose to leave. 'I'm so glad we've met again,' he said. I went slowly downstairs, certain he had had something to say. A door opened on the ground floor and a gentle voice said, 'I'm afraid, sir, that Dr Candy is sadly changed.' It was Ezra Jennings.

Chapter 7   Lost Memory

He had a patient to see and was going my way. As we were leaving Fritzinghall I told him that Dr Candy had tried to tell me something but his memory had failed him. 'Is there a way I might possibly help him to remember?' I asked.

His dreamy brown eyes looked at me with a flash of interest. 'It's amazing he's still alive,' he said. 'The fever did permanent damage. However, Mr Blake, it may be possible to trace Dr Candy's lost memory without Dr Candy.' He stopped to pick a wild flower. 'How beautiful it is,' he said. His sudden joy surprised me. He turned to me, the smile leaving his face. 'I'll explain, Mr Blake. During the worst part of his fever he was delirious, talking endlessly. I never left him as long as his life was in danger. To pass those terrible hours at his bedside I wrote down what he said, leaving spaces between his broken, seemingly unconnected phrases. It became a kind of game, trying to put the pieces together, guessing, working out the missing links. One night he mentioned your name several times.'

'Let's go back immediately and look at your notes!' I said.

He shook his head. 'Impossible, Mr Blake. He was my patient, therefore, I'm afraid, it's a medical secret – despite the fact that I believe he was talking to *you*.'

I decided to tell him the whole truth. I told him I was suspected of stealing the diamond, and why, and that Dr Candy's memory could perhaps clear my name. He listened patiently, even anxiously. 'I'm sorry to disappoint you, Mr Blake,' he said as we reached a fork in the road, 'but not one word about the diamond ever crossed his lips.'

'It's certain I took the diamond,' I said, 'but I did it without my own knowledge. I have to be able to prove that somehow.' He became suddenly still, looked at me very strangely, then took me by the arm. 'You have travelled in the East, Mr Blake. You must know about the effects of opium on human consciousness?' I nodded. He invited me to sit down on a wall.

'I must now tell *you* a secret,' he said. 'Look at my face. Can you believe I'm forty years old? No, obviously. My life is near its end, Mr Blake. For ten years I've suffered from an incurable disease of the nerves. Without opium the indescribable pain of it would – should have killed me long ago. Yes, it is a powerful pain killer but even opium has its limit . . .' As he spoke, I realized the horror his daily life must have been. 'Were your nerves out of order this time last year?' he asked me. 'Were you restless, or nervous?' I told him I was, that I had been sleeping badly night after night. 'Was the night of the birthday an exception? Try and remember.' I told him it was the first night I had slept well since I had given up smoking – the cause of my nervousness. He let go of my arm, as though at last seeing something. 'I'm absolutely certain of one thing,' he said slowly. 'I know what Dr Candy wanted to say to you. I have it in the notes I took at his bedside.'

'Explain yourself!' I cried. 'Please, what do you mean?'

'I have a patient to see. Give me two hours, then call at Dr Candy's house.' He hurried away.

Chapter 8   Opium

I returned to Fritzinghall. Two hours later Ezra Jennings was waiting for me, sitting alone in a little bare room on the ground floor, the walls covered with illustrations of horrible diseases. 'I have my notes ready for you,' he said. 'But before we start, do you mind if I ask you one or two more questions?'

'Ask me anything you like!' I replied.

'Do you remember having an argument with Dr Candy at the birthday dinner – on the subject of his profession?' All that I could remember was that I had stupidly and repeatedly attacked the art of medicine – enough to anger even Dr Candy. 'Did you have any special anxiety about the diamond at that time?' he asked.

'Yes. I knew it was the object of a conspiracy. I was extremely worried about its safety.' I told him about the three Indians.

He handed me his notes. 'Read that in the light of my two questions,' he said. 'You'll see not only that you took the diamond but that you did it in a state of trance. You will also see that Dr Candy gave you a dose of opium without you knowing – to disprove your stupid theories and to teach you a lesson. If he hadn't fallen ill, he would have returned the next day and acknowledged the trick he played on you. Miss Verinder would have heard about it and the truth would have been discovered immediately. The opium was secretly given to you in some way.

Now, read Dr Candy's words, which like a puzzle, I have completed with my own, in capitals.'

I read them:

I decided (TO TEACH) Mr Blake (A) lesson. He (SAYS HE) can't sleep. (I) told him (HIS NERVES ARE) out of order. (HE) said (MEDICINE IS) like a blind man (SEARCHING IN THE) dark. (I TOLD) him medicine can (EASILY CURE) sleeplessness. (I GAVE HIM) forty drops (OF OPIUM) without him knowing. (I WILL TELL) him tomorrow morning.

'Now!' he said. 'Do you believe you were acting under the influence of opium?'

'Yes,' I said, shaken by what I had read. 'I'm beginning to think I must have been. But how does that help? How can I prove it?'

'Are you willing to try a daring experiment?' he asked.

'Tell me what to do!' I said impatiently.

'Do this,' he said. 'Steal the diamond, unconsciously, in a trance, for a second time, and in the presence of witnesses.' He ignored my laughter. 'It can be done! Listen, there is medical evidence to prove that everything we think is recorded by the brain and can be recalled later – but we have absolutely no memory or knowledge of this. It is subconscious. Do you understand?' I nodded. 'Now, the common belief is that opium sends you to sleep. This is only half true. I'm speaking to you now under the influence of opium. It makes you lively and awake immediately after it has been taken, then, later, it has a calming influence. The first effect produces rich impressions in your mind, extraordinarily clear thoughts – your fears and doubts about the diamond, for instance, were exaggerated into certainties that pulled you to Miss Verinder's sitting-room. Later, back in your room, as the second, calming action took effect, you fell into a deep sleep. The experiment may enable you to remember what you did with the diamond after you left Miss Verinder's room. You may remember where you hid it.'

I stopped him there. 'The diamond is in London now,' I said. 'And nobody knows how it got there.' I told him about Luker.

'All right,' he said. 'But the experiment may still throw some light on how the stone got into someone else's hands. In order for it to succeed it is extremely important to recreate exactly the same conditions as on the birthday night.'

'Out of the question,' I said. 'Lady Verinder is dead. Mr Ablewhite is in Europe...'

'That doesn't matter! No, no, what I meant was that you must give up smoking again. You must be in exactly the same nervous state. And of course everything in the house must be the same as on the night of the birthday.'

'Perhaps, but it's Rachel's house now. She'll never agree to it.'

'Let me write to her,' he said. 'I'll tell her every thing.' He pressed my hand gently. 'What do you think?'

I agreed.

It was then the 15th of June. The experiment has now been tried. I will now pass the pen to Ezra Jennings. He will tell you the result.

FOURTH NARRATIVE

From the Diary of Ezra Jennings

1849 – June 15th. Terrible pain all day. I wrote a letter to Miss Verinder.

June 16th – Woke late after a terrible night – yesterday's opium produced awful nightmares. A return of the pain at dawn. It was late morning before I could visit Mr Blake. He had had a very restless night. 'Exactly what happened last year when I gave up smoking!' he complained. I advised him to get some fresh air. He told me he had written to Mr Bruff, his lawyer. I left him to go and see my patients, feeling oddly happy. I feel such a contrast between the way this charming young man treats me and the merciless distrust of everyone else. Everyone except poor Dr Candy, of course. I owe him everything.

June 17th – In the night, Death came whispering around my bed again. Miss Verinder's reply arrived in the morning. A charming letter! She sees no need for the experiment, saying my letter is proof enough for her that Mr Blake is innocent. She even blames herself for not having suspected some kind of trick before! Nevertheless, she asks me to tell him that we have her permission to use the house for the experiment. She has written to Mr Betteredge, asking him to prepare the house, and even offers to be one of the witnesses. I believe she wants to be there to tell him, before he goes through with the experiment, that she loves him and that there is no need to prove himself. She declares that she has always loved him, even during the last year. Is it possible that you, Ezra Jennings, before you go, may bring these two fine young people back together?

Two o'clock – I have just returned from my medical visits. Mr Blake's condition is the same: a night of broken sleep, loss of appetite, nervousness. I told him everything he needed to know about Miss Verinder's reply. 'She agrees simply out of common politeness!' he replied. 'But she keeps her own opinion.'

Five o'clock – I have written to Miss Verinder.

June 18th – More horrible pain in the early morning. I had to return to the opium for the hundredth time. It was one o'clock before I could drag myself to the hotel. Mr Betteredge was with Mr Blake when I arrived. Mr Blake had slept badly again. He had received a letter from Mr Bruff, saying he totally disapproves of the experiment, and that he could see better magic shows in

London. But Mr Blake was determined to go through with the experiment. I discussed the preparations with Mr Betteredge. It isn't going to be easy — the house has been shut up for a year.

June 19th — A letter from Miss Verinder, agreeing to my arrangements.

June 20th — Mr Blake was extremely nervous — he is now continually restless at night. Sergeant Cuff wrote to him from Ireland saying that because of Lady Verinder's generosity towards him he agrees to help Mr Franklin in any way he can. I advised him to inform the Sergeant of everything that had happened and invite him to be present during the experiment.

June 21st — Mr Blake has had his worst night yet.

June 22nd — The house will be ready tomorrow. There is nothing to do now except wait until Monday and watch Mr Blake carefully. I was glad to hear that Mr Bruff has agreed to come. He is strongly against the experiment and therefore will be a valuable witness. If we convince him we can convince anyone.

June 24th — Mr Blake and I went for a drive today. The fresh air calmed both our nerves. I had more terrible pain last night.

June 25th, Monday — At last! The day of the experiment.

Seven o'clock — We're now going to eat. After dinner I'm going to make conversation about the Moonstone. When I've filled his mind with it I'll give him the first dose. My notes inform me that Dr Candy gave him forty drops — quite a large amount.

Ten o'clock — Miss Verinder and Mr Bruff arrived together an hour ago. She was shocked, of course, by my appearance, but she hid it better than most. 'I can't treat you like a stranger, Mr Jennings,' she said warmly. 'Your letters have made me so happy.' I felt a wave of pleasure go through me. 'Where is he now?' she asked. I told her I had already accompanied him to his room. She went straight to hers. I went upstairs to Mr Blake.

'When are you going to give me the opium?' he asked. It was not yet ten o'clock. Dr Candy could not have possibly given him the dose before eleven. I told him I would keep him company until then. We talked for a while and now I sit writing while he reads a novel. It is now nearly eleven. I'm so excited that not even the pain affects me!

Two o'clock a.m. – The experiment is now over. This is what happened. At eleven I rang the bell for Betteredge and told Mr Blake to get ready for bed. Betteredge and I went and knocked on Mr Bruff's bedroom door. I asked the lawyer to be present when I prepared the opium, and then remain with us in Mr Blake's room. He agreed reluctantly, saying he had more important things to do, making a show of gathering up his legal papers. We then went to see Miss Verinder.

She was pale and restless, striding up and down. She asked me how he was, how long the opium would take to work. I said roughly an hour. She agreed to wait in her bedroom, exactly as before. I measured out the dose, mixed it with water, then got out the piece of glass that was to be the diamond. She showed me the drawer to put it in. Betteredge and Bruff witnessed everything. We then left Miss Verinder and returned to Mr Blake. They saw me give him the dose and tell him to lie down and wait. We sat down to wait with him. I encouraged Mr Blake to talk to me, always bringing the conversation back to the diamond. We talked about bringing it from London, the Indians, putting it in the bank in Fritzinghall, taking it out again. Little by little the opium began to do its work. His eyes began to shine, sweat appeared on his forehead. Gradually his talk lost its sense. Finally, he became silent. Then suddenly he sat up in bed. Ten minutes passed. Nothing happened. He began to talk to himself.

At twenty past twelve he put one leg out of bed and said, 'I wish I'd never taken it out of the bank. The Indians may be hidden in the house. How can I sleep? – the diamond isn't even locked up.' He got up, then – to my surprise – lay down again. I had a horrible feeling the experiment had failed, but then he slowly got up again. We waited, hidden behind the curtains. He crossed the room, opened the door and went out.

We followed him along the corridor. Without looking back, he went straight to Miss Verinder's rooms, opened her sitting-room door and went in. He went to the middle of the room and looked round him. The door of Miss Verinder's bedroom was slightly open. I could see the dim outline of her white dress just inside.

After a minute he went to the Indian cabinet, opened drawers and found the diamond. He took it out and stood still again. What would he do next? Would he leave the room and show us what he did with the diamond when he had returned to his room? No. He let the diamond drop out of his hand. It fell by the door, visible to him and to us. For a long time he looked down at it emptily, until suddenly his head sank down on to his chest. It was too late. The calming action of the drug had begun.

'It's all over,' I said. 'He'll probably sleep for the next six hours.' We gathered around him. 'He can sleep here on the sofa,' Miss Verinder said. 'I'll watch over him.' We placed him on the sofa, and for the rest of the night she and I kept watch over him in silence. The light of day grew in the room and still he never moved. Towards six I felt my pain coming back and made an excuse to leave the room. Luckily, it was not a long attack, and I was soon able to return.

It is now eight o'clock. He will soon wake up. I am going to leave them alone together.

Eleven o'clock – The house is empty again. They all went back to London by the ten o'clock train.

Mr Blake will write and tell me what happens in London. Miss Verinder has invited me to stay here in the autumn when they return – for their marriage, no doubt. My patients are waiting so I must hurry.

FIFTH NARRATIVE

The story continued by Franklin Blake

I woke that morning ignorant of what I had said or done after the drug first took effect. I opened my eyes and looked into Rachel's.

When we arrived in London, a boy called Gooseberry met Bruff at the station. After listening to him, Bruff said he had to leave immediately on important business. He pulled me to a taxi and told the driver to hurry to Lombard Street. 'News of Luker,' he said. 'He was seen leaving his house accompanied by two policemen in plain clothes.'

Gooseberry came into the crowded bank with us. Two men came up to Bruff as soon as we entered. 'Have you seen him?' asked the lawyer. They said Luker had arrived half an hour ago and gone into an inner office. 'Let's wait then,' Bruff said.

I couldn't see any Indians anywhere. 'They must have a spy here,' Bruff said. Gooseberry pulled on his coat. Luker was leaving an office with his two guards. 'Watch him,' Bruff whispered. 'If he passes the stone to anyone he will do it here.' Luker went straight to the door without noticing us. In the crowd I saw his hand move suddenly as he passed a short, fat man. At the door his guards placed themselves on either side of him. They left, followed closely by one of Bruff's men.

I pointed out the man to Bruff. 'Did you see anything?' I said. He shook his head. Neither Bruff's second man nor Gooseberry were anywhere to be seen. 'What do we do now?' I asked.

'Come back to my office and wait,' he replied. Bruff's second man was waiting there when we arrived. 'I'm sorry, sir,' he said. 'I was sure I saw him pass something to an elderly gentleman. It turns out he's a respectable doctor in Westminster.'

Bruff asked him where Gooseberry was. He didn't know.

As we were having supper at Bruff's office, the man who followed Luker returned. Luker had gone straight home and not gone out again. His guards had left later. 'He would never have sent them home if he had the stone,' said Bruff. The house was being carefully watched. There had been no sign of the Indians.

We waited until it was time for Bruff to go home. I returned to Rachel, leaving my address in case the boy returned.

When I got home after midnight my servant informed me that Gooseberry had called. He would return early the next day.

As I was having breakfast there was a knock on my door. Expecting Gooseberry, I was surprised when Sergeant Cuff entered. 'I got back from Ireland last night,' he said.

'I presume you've come to get back your reputation,' I said.

'I admit I made a mess of the case,' he replied unwillingly. 'But no, sir, I have come to return Lady Verinder's great generosity.'

I told him everything. To my surprise he took Ezra Jennings's trance theory extremely seriously. He agreed with Jennings that I must have taken the stone back to my room, but not that I had hidden it there. 'Well, what did I do then?' I asked.

'Don't you have any idea?' he replied. I shook my head. He went to my desk, wrote something and put the paper in an envelope. 'Open this when you know the truth,' he said. 'I made a mistake last year, but not this year.' I put the letter in my pocket. 'Now,' he said, 'let's wait and see if "Gooseberry" turns up.'

Gooseberry arrived at ten o'clock. As soon as he heard Cuff's name his huge eyes never left the famous detective. 'Come, my lad,' said the Sergeant, 'tell us all. Where did you go?'

'I followed a tall man with a black beard, dressed like a sailor. He left the bank in a hurry and called a taxi. I ran after it and hung on behind.' Bruff's secretary arrived at this point and I had to leave the room. Before I could return Cuff came hurrying out with Gooseberry. 'Quick!' Cuff said. 'Get a taxi immediately!'

Five minutes later we were on our way east, with Gooseberry explaining to me what happened. 'The taxi went to the Port of London, sir. The sailor with the black beard got out and spoke to an officer of the Rotterdam steamboat. It was leaving next morning and no passengers could come on board until then. Then he left the port. In the street, I noticed a man dressed like a mechanic walking on the opposite side of the road, watching the sailor. The sailor went into an eating-house. I waited outside, watching the mechanic. After a minute, a taxi stopped next to him. A dark-faced person inside spoke to him. Then the taxi moved slowly on down the street and the mechanic crossed the road and went into the eating-house. I waited a bit then went in after him. I only had two pence, sir, but I had a good meal!'

'What did you see in the eating-house?' I asked.

'The sailor reading a newspaper at one table, the mechanic reading a newspaper at another. It was dusk before the sailor got up and left, looking suspiciously around him out in the street. He didn't seem sure about where to go next. Me and the mechanic followed him to Lower Thames Street where he stopped in front of a pub, "The Wheel of Fortune". I followed him in, followed by the mechanic. It was very crowded. The sailor asked for a bed. No, the landlord said, they were full. A barmaid corrected him: Room Ten was empty. I noticed, just before a waiter took the sailor upstairs to his room, that the mechanic had disappeared. I waited. The landlord was called for. I heard angry voices upstairs. The mechanic appeared at the top of the stairs, looking very drunk. The landlord pulled him downstairs, arguing with him, and threw him out. It seems he'd been discovered in Number

Ten. I noticed that as soon as he was outside he wasn't drunk anymore. I waited. Nothing else happened, so I decided to go back to Mr Bruff's office. As I left I noticed the mechanic on the other side of the street, staring up at a lit window in the roof.'

'The Indians didn't risk being seen at the bank,' said Cuff. 'They employed someone else. In "The Wheel of Fortune" their man hears the number of the sailor's room (the Indians would certainly want a description of the room). He was found in the room when the sailor went up, and pretended to be drunk. As for what happened after Gooseberry left . . . we can only hope.'

When we entered 'The Wheel of Fortune' it was clear that something was wrong. The barmaid said the landlord was upstairs and was not to be bothered. Sergeant Cuff ignored this and went up. The barmaid called out and the landlord, obviously in a temper, appeared in front of us at the top of the stairs. The words 'I am Sergeant Cuff,' had a magical effect. 'I have some enquiries to make, sir,' said the Sergeant, 'about a dark man dressed as a sailor who slept here last night.'

'Good God!' exclaimed the landlord. 'That's the man who's upsetting the whole house at the moment.'

'Can we see him, please?' asked the Sergeant.

'Nobody's been able to see him since seven this morning — that was the time he asked to be called. The door's locked, there's been no reply from inside —'

'Could he leave the room in any way other than the door?' interrupted the Sergeant.

'The room is under the roof. There's a window, leading on to the roof . . . You don't think he's left without paying, Sergeant, do you?' As he spoke, a carpenter arrived to open the door.

It wasn't easy — a piece of furniture had been placed against it inside. When the door was finally pushed open we saw the man, dressed, lying on the bed inside with a pillow over his face.

Sergeant Cuff removed it. The man's coffee-coloured face was perfectly calm, his eyes wide open. He was dead. I felt a soft pull on my coat-tail. 'Look, sir!' whispered Gooseberry, pointing to a little wooden box, open, empty. There was a torn sheet of paper inside, with the Lombard Street Bank's name on it.

Inside this envelope is a small wooden box containing an extremely valuable object, left in the bank's care by Mr Septimus Luker. The box can only be removed from the bank by Mr Luker himself, and by no other person.

'The man's face is disguised,' said Cuff. 'Look!' He pointed to a thin line of white just below the man's hair. 'Let's see what's under this,' he said, taking a handful of the man's hair. My nerves were not strong enough. I had to turn away.

'He's pulled off his hair!' whispered Gooseberry. There was a pause, then a cry of astonishment from the landlord. Cuff asked him for water and a towel. 'He's washing off his face!' the boy went on. I heard footsteps. Cuff appeared beside me.

'Before you look round, sir,' he said, 'open the envelope I gave you this morning.' I opened it. 'Read the name, Mr Blake, written inside.' I read the name, looked round, and saw him lying on the bed, half of his make-up washed off. It was Godfrey Ablewhite.

SIXTH NARRATIVE

Contributed by Sergeant Cuff

First of all, what happened to the diamond? The letter I received from Mr Murthwaite yesterday leaves little doubt. Writing from India, the explorer informed me that a new temple of the Moon-God is being built in Benares. The work began shortly after the arrival of three priests in the city, and is being organized by them. At a ceremony to bless the site of the temple, the three men announced that 'The Eye of the Moon has returned.'

The man's coffee-coloured face was perfectly calm, his eyes wide open. He was dead.

As for the dead man, later investigations revealed that Mr Ablewhite's life had two sides: side A (the public one) shows a gentleman of considerable reputation as a speaker at charitable meetings, a man of great administrative abilities, who managed various charitable societies; side B (the hidden one) reveals a man of pleasure with a fine house in the suburbs (not bought in his name), and with a woman (not with his name either) living in luxury in that house – surrounded by pictures by great artists, jewels, the finest horses and carriages, all worth a small fortune – somebody else's fortune. Which brings us to Mr Godfrey Ablewhite's motive for stealing the Moonstone.

My investigations revealed that as a lawyer he had been trusted to take care of twenty thousand pounds, belonging to a young gentleman, an orphan. The young man would inherit the whole sum on his eighteenth birthday, in February 1850. Until then, Mr Godfrey, had to continue paying him six hundred pounds half-yearly (on Midsummer's day and on Christmas Day). The motive was simple. Exactly as Mr Bruff suspected: he needed money (a lot of money) quickly.

Mr Ablewhite's father informed me that the day before Miss Verinder's birthday (two days before Midsummer's day) his son asked him for a loan of three hundred pounds. Mr Ablewhite refused. Godfrey Ablewhite had had to find three hundred pounds by the 24th June, and twenty thousand pounds by the following February. Otherwise he was a ruined man.

The following night, Dr Candy played Mr Franklin a little practical joke. He trusted the administration of the dose of opium to Ablewhite (the lawyer confessed to this in circumstances which I will come to later). You will remember Ablewhite (who had also suffered from Mr Blake's tongue that evening) joined Betteredge in trying to persuade Mr Blake to take a little whisky before bed. Let us now direct our attention to Luker's house in London.

Late on the evening of 23rd June 1848, Luker received a visit from Ablewhite. You can imagine his surprise when Ablewhite produced the Moonstone. Luker was extremely curious to know how the famous stone had come into the lawyer's possession. Ablewhite told a story which only sharpened Luker's suspicion. Desperate, Ablewhite finally told the truth.

His money troubles had kept him awake on the night of the birthday. He had heard Blake talking to himself in his bedroom and had looked in to see what was the matter. He saw Blake, candle in hand, coming towards the door. He followed Blake to Miss Verinder's sitting-room, saw him take the diamond, and also saw Miss Verinder watching from her bedroom. Blake returned to his bedroom with the diamond, and the next morning had forgotten everything that happened.

The next morning, Miss Verinder's behaviour showed that she had decided to remain silent. Waiting to see what would happen that morning, Ablewhite gradually realized he could keep the diamond – without any fear of being suspected. The Moonstone stood between him and ruin. It didn't take him long to make up his mind. He went to London and made a deal with Luker, and with the money, saved himself.

When Mr Ablewhite went abroad after inheriting five thousand pounds from the old lady, he went to Amsterdam. I have discovered from the Dutch police that he made arrangements for a diamond to be cut up into smaller stones, at a later date. Strangely, it was that five thousand pounds that led Ablewhite to his death because it enabled him to pay back Luker and recover the Moonstone.

I will only add one more detail to Mr Blake's description of the circumstances of Ablewhite's death. The lock of the window in the roof was broken – no doubt by the 'mechanic' – so enabling a trained, athletic person to open it from the outside, descend noiselessly and . . . I will leave the rest to your imagination.

ACTIVITIES

Pages 1–16

Before you read

1 Look at the Word List at the back of the book. Complete the sentences with one of the words on the list.

   a The struggling man sank deeper and deeper into the ....

   b .... was used to relieve pain in the past.

   c 'Thank God he's safe!' she ....

   d The chapter contains both description and ....

   e The man has a .... leg and cannot walk properly.

   f In his ...., my grandfather gave me £25,000.

   g There's a .... of wet paint on your jacket.

2 Read the Introduction and answer these questions.

   a What is the Moonstone in this novel?

   b When was the novel written?

   c In what way was this novel very new?

   d What is unusual about the way the story is told?

While you read

3 Who:

   a kills three priests in order to obtain
      the Moonstone from the Palace of
      Seringapatam?   ....

   b agrees to write about the loss of the
      diamond?   ....

   c returns from abroad?   ....

   d is planning to harm Franklin Blake?   ....

   e is a housemaid and had been a thief?   ....

   f has the Moonstone now?   ....

   g will receive the Moonstone on June 21st?   ....

   h is a very good-looking lawyer?   ....

   i suspects Colonel Herncastle's motives
      for giving the Moonstone to Rachel?   ....

4 Explain why:

    a the Moonstone is so important.

    b the three Indian men come to Lady Verinder's house.

    c Colonel Herncastle gave the Moonstone to Rachel.

    d Franklin Blake takes the Moonstone to the bank.

    e Rosanna acts strangely.

    f a French lawyer visited Franklin.

    g Franklin sleeps badly.

    h Rachel screams when she sees the diamond.

5 Describe:

    a Franklin and his relationship with Rachel.

    b Godfrey Ablewhite and his relationship with Rachel.

    c Rosanna and her relationship with Betteredge.

6 Answer these questions. Give reasons for your answers.

    a Do you think that Franklin should have warned Rachel and Lady Verinder about the three Indians?

    b Which character do you like best?

Pages 16–31

Before you read

7 Do you think the Indians will make an attempt to steal the diamond? If so, how?

While you read

8 Complete the sentences with one or two words.

    a The Indians see the Moonstone on Rachel's ....

    b .... screams that the diamond has been stolen.

    c It has been proved that the .... remained in their hotel all night.

    d Superintendent Seegrave finds a smear in the paint on Rachel's .... door.

    e The paint on the door dried at about .... on Thursday.

f Sergeant Cuff doesn't think .... stole the diamond.

g Sergeant Cuff says they must find the .... that made the smear on the door.

h Some servants heard the sounds of a .... at four in the morning in Rosanna's room.

i Cuff learns that Rosanna went to Fritzinghall to buy some .... to make a ....

After you read

9 Answer the questions.

    a Who were the guests at the party who were described by Betteredge? Briefly describe them.

    b Why does Cuff think that the paint smear is so important?

    c How does Rachel behave after the theft of the diamond?

10 Work with another student. Have this conversation.

    Student A: You are Betteridge. Explain to Penelope why it seems clear that Rosanna helped with the disappearance of the diamond.

    Student B: You are Penelope. Listen to your father, ask questions and offer your opinion.

11 Answer the questions. Give reasons for your opinions.

    a Why does Cuff say, 'Nobody has stolen the diamond.'?

    b Do you agree with Cuff?

    c What do you think Rosanna intends to do with the case she bought from Mrs Yolland?

Pages 32–44

Before you read

12 Look at the chapter titles. What do you think will happen next?

While you read

13 Put these sentences in the right order, from 1–7.

    a Limping Lucy says she has a letter from Rosanna.   .....

    b Cuff explains his suspicions to Lady Verinder.   .....

    c Cuff says he thinks Rachel stole her own diamond.   .....

d Mr Septimus Lukus is annoyed by three Indians.   .....

e Cuff discovers that Rosanna has killed herself.   .....

f Cuff leaves.   .....

g Rachel goes to stay in Fritzinghall.   .....

After you read

14 Who says these things? Who to? Explain the situation.

    a 'I want to be in the way.'

    b 'Mr Franklin has hurt her cruelly without intending it.'

    c 'What the sand gets, the sand keeps forever!'

    d 'This is your fault!'

    e 'Time will tell if I am right or wrong.'

    f 'The Moonstone has given Colonel Herncastle his revenge.'

    g '*He* caused her death!'

15 Explain why Cuff thinks that Rachel is hiding the diamond.

16 Answer these questions. Give reasons for your answers.

    a Do you think Cuff is right about Rachel?

    b How do you feel about Rosanna's death? Was it obvious she was going to kill herself?

Pages 45–54

Before you read

17 Which of these events do you think will happen?

    a The Indians will obtain the diamond.

    b A character in the story will die.

    c There will be news of the diamond.

    d Rachel will marry.

    e A main character will be attacked.

While you read

18 Are these sentences right (✓) or wrong (✗)?

    a Franklin pays Miss Clack to describe events in London.   .....

    b Miss Clack has lunch with the Verinders.   .....

    c Godfrey and Mr Luker have a discussion at a bank.   .....

    d Some Indians steal a book from Godfrey Ablewhite.   .....

e Rachel asks Godfrey to tell her about the Indians. .....

f Rachel says she knows Godfrey didn't take the diamond. .....

g Lady Verinder tells Miss Clack that she has heart disease but will live until she is old. .....

h Lady Verinder gives Miss Clack a present. .....

i Miss Clack hides in the Verinder's living-room. .....

After you read

19 Briefly describe in your own words:

   a the attack on Godfrey by the Indians.

   b Rachel and Godfrey's conversation about the attack.

   c the conversation between Miss Clack and Mr Bruff.

20 Mr Bruff tells Miss Clack: 'All we know is that the Moonstone came to London, and that Mr Luker or his banker has it at the moment.' How do we know this?

21 Answer these questions. Give reasons for your opinions.

   a Rachel cries, 'I know who took the Moonstone?' What does this tell us about her? How do you think she knows?

   b Are you confused about who stole the Moonstone?

Pages 55–67

Before you read

22 At the end of page 54, Godfrey Ablewhite says, 'Do it today, you must do it today.' What do you think he must do?

While you read

23 Underline the wrong word(s) in each sentence and write the right word(s).

   a Rachel accepts Godfrey's offer of friendship. ....

   b Lady Verinder gets better. ....

   c Rachel goes to stay with Miss Clack. ....

   d Godfrey is not happy when Rachel changes her mind about marrying him. ....

   e Mrs Ablewhite becomes very angry with Rachel. ....

f Rachel learns that Godfrey offered to
marry her because he loved her. ....

g An Indian visits Mr Bruff and asks him
for the diamond. ....

h Mr Bruff predicts that the Indians will try
and obtain the Moonstone in June 1849. ....

After you read

24 Describe the role that these people play in these chapters.

    a Godfrey Ablewhite

    b Mr Bruff

25 Explain why Mr Bruff ends his narrative with these words: *June
1849 – expect news of Indians towards the end of the month.*

26 Describe Miss Clack. In what ways does Collins make her an
amusing character?

27 What is your opinion of Godfrey Ablewhite, and why? Can you
understand why Rachel agreed to marry him?

Pages 68–85

Before you read

28 Look at the chapter titles. Answer these questions.

    a What do you think will happen when Franklin returns?

    b What do you think the chapter called *The Letter* is about?

While you read

29 Put the events in the right order, from 1–7.

    a Franklin learns that Godfrey has received some
money from a rich old lady. .....

    b Rachel tells Franklin she saw him take the diamond. .....

    c Franklin reads Rosanna's letter explaining why she
did not destroy the nightgown. .....

    d Franklin reads Rosanna's note giving him directions. .....

    e Franklin visits Dr Candy. .....

    f Rachel refuses to see Franklin. .....

    g Franklin finds a nightgown with his name on it. .....

After you read

30 Answer these questions.

    a What does Rosanna's note give directions for?

    b When Franklin sees the name on the nightgown, why is he so shocked?

    c What persuaded Rosanna that Franklin was the thief?

    d Why didn't Rosanna destroy the nightgown?

    e In order to prove that Franklin took the diamond, what other proof must there be, according to Mr Bruff?

    f What does Mr Bruff say that Franklin must do in order to regain Rachel?

    g How has Dr Candy changed?

31 Work with another student. Have this conversation.

    Student A: You are Rachel. Describe what happened on the night the Moonstone was stolen. Talk about your meeting with Franklin and your feelings for him.

    Student B: You are Rachel's best friend. Listen, ask questions and give your opinion.

32 What do you think is the explanation for Franklin's name on the nightgown?

Pages 85–101

Before you read

33 Answer these questions. What do you think?

    a What does Dr Candy want to tell Franklin?

    b What will the Indians do in the last part of the story?

While you read

34 Complete the sentences with one or two words.

    a While Dr Candy was very ill, he mentioned .... name several times.

    b Ezra Jenning shows Franklin proof that Dr Candy gave Franklin ....

    c Jennings and Franklin decide to try an ....

    d Rachel realizes that Franklin is ....

    e During the experiment, Franklin finds the diamond and then
       .... it.

    f At the bank, Gooseberry follows a tall man dressed like a
       ....

    g Cuff discovers that the sailor is in fact ....

    h The person who killed Godfrey looked like a ....

After you read

35 Explain:

    a the role of Dr Candy in the theft of the Moonstone.

    b how Ezra Jennings knows this.

    c why the experiment is disappointing.

    d what happens to the diamond in the end.

    e how the Indians get the Moonstone back.

36 Look back through the novel and describe the role of the Indians
in the story.

37 Answer these questions. Give reasons for your opinion.

    a Do you think Godfrey deserves his death?

    b Did the explanation for the theft of the diamond surprise
you?

Writing

38 *The Moonstone* is often described as one of the best English
detective novels. What is your opinion of it as a detective story?
Give reasons for your opinion.

39 Who is the most interesting character in the book? Why? Give
reasons for your answer.

40 Write a newspaper report describing either the theft of the
Moonstone or the murder of Godfrey Ablewhite.

41 This story is seen through the eyes of different people. How
does this contribute to the way the story unfolds and to our
understanding of it?

42 This book was very popular when it was first written, and it has
remained popular since. What do you think are the qualities that
have kept the story fresh? What is it about *The Moonstone* that
still appeals to us today?

43 *The Moonstone* has been made into a film and produced as a stage play. Which parts of the book do you think would be most difficult to present on stage? What changes could be made in order to overcome the problems?

44 Which scene do you think is the most powerful or dramatic? Explain why.

45 After Ezra Jennings realizes that Dr Candy had given Franklin opium, he says he will write to Rachel, explaining everything and asking her to agree to the experiment that will recreate the same conditions as on the birthday night. Write this letter.

46 Could today's methods of crime investigation have solved the mystery more quickly? If so, how?

47 Tell the story of the novel briefly from the point of view of Rachel.

WORD LIST

bow (v) to bend the top part of your body forward in order to show respect for someone important

cabinet (n) a piece of furniture with doors and shelves or drawers, used for storing or showing things

charitable (adj) intending to give help to people who are poor or less fortunate than yourself

colonel (n) a high level officer in the army

committee (n) a group of people chosen to meet together in order to make decisions or do a special job

conspiracy (n) a secret plan made by two or more people to do something that is harmful or illegal

deformed (adj) the wrong shape, especially because it has grown or developed wrongly

dose (n) the amount of a medicine or a drug that you should take

exclaim (v) to say something suddenly and loudly because you are surprised, angry, or excited

fascinated (adj) extremely interested

inherit (v) to receive money, property etc from someone after they have died

ladyship (n) '*your ladyship*' is used instead of '*madam*' when speaking to a woman who has the title of *Lady*

limp (v) to walk unevenly or with difficulty because something is wrong with one leg or one foot

maid (n) a female servant, especially in a large house or hotel

narrative (n) a description of events in a story

nightgown (n) a nightdress

opium (n) a powerful illegal drug made from seeds. Other drugs made from opium are used to reduce severe pain

Oriental (adj) from or about the eastern part of the world

pawn (v) to give something valuable in exchange for a loan until the loan is repaid

quicksand (n) wet sand that is dangerous because you can sink down into it

relieved (adj) feeling happy because you are no longer worried about something

sigh (v) to breathe out making a long sound, especially because you are bored, disappointed, tired etc

smear (n/v) a dirty mark made by a small amount of something spread across a surface

stubborn (adj) determined not to change, even when people think you should

Superintendent (n) an important officer in the British police

telegram (n) a message sent electrically by wire

temple (n) a religious building in non-Christian and non-Muslim religions

terrace (n) a flat outdoor area next to a building or on a roof, where you can sit outside

uneasy (adj) worried or slightly afraid because you think that something bad might happen

will (n) a legal document that says who will receive your money and property after you die

The Woman in White
Wilkie Collins

Only the Woman in White knows the truth of Laura Fairlie's cruel husband. Can Walter Hartwright discover the terrible secret? From the moment Walter meets this mysterious woman, his future and that of Laura are linked forever.

Great Expectations
Charles Dickens

Pip is a poor orphan whose life is changed for ever by two very different meetings – one with an escaped convict and the other with an eccentric old lady and the beautiful girl who lives with her. And who is the mysterious person who leaves him a fortune?

Oliver Twist
Charles Dickens

His mother is dead, so little Oliver Twist is brought up in the workhouse. Beaten and starved, he runs away to London, where he joins Fagin's gang of thieves. By chance he also finds good new friends – but can they protect him from people who rob and murder without mercy?

Crime and Punishment
Fyodor Dostoevsky

Raskolnikoff, a young student, has been forced to give up his
university studies because of lack of money. He withdraws from
society and, poor and lonely, he develops a plan to murder a
greedy old moneylender. Surely the murder of one worthless old
woman would be excused, even approved of, if it made possible a
thousand good deeds? But this crime is just the beginning of the
story. Afterwards he must go on a journey of self-discovery. He
must try to understand his motives and explain them to others. Can
he succeed?

The Testament
John Grisham

Nate O'Riley is a powerful Washington lawyer. Returning to work
after a long stay in hospital is difficult for Nate. Then he is sent on
a journey that takes him from the tense courtrooms of Washington
to the dangerous swamps of Brazil. It is a journey that will change
his life forever . . . *Another great thriller from John Grisham, one of
the world's most popular writers.*

Snow Falling on Cedars
David Guterson

It is 1954 and Kabuo Miyamoto is on trial for murder. He is a
Japanese American living on the island of San Piedro, off the
north-west coast of America. The Second World War has left an
atmosphere of anger and suspicion in this small community. Will
Kabuo receive a fair trial? And will the true cause of the victim's
death be discovered?

*There are hundreds of Penguin Readers to choose from – world classics,
film adaptations, modern-day crime and adventure, short stories,
biographies, American classics, non-fiction, plays ...*

For a complete list of all Penguin Readers titles, please contact your local
Pearson Longman office or visit our website.

www.penguinreaders.com

Les Misérables
Victor Hugo

Jean Valjean is free at last after nineteen years in prison. Cold and hungry, he is rejected by everyone he meets. But Jean's life is changed forever when he discovers love. He spends the rest of his life helping people, like himself, who have been victims of poverty and social injustice – 'les misérables'.

Captain Corelli's Mandolin
Louis de Bernières

Louis de Bernières is one of the best writers in English today.

This is a great love story set in the tragedy of war. It is 1941. The Italian officer, Captain Corelli, falls in love with Pelagia, a young Greek girl. But Pelegia's fiancé is fighting the Italian army . . .

Captain Corelli's Mandolin is now a film, starring Nicholas Cage.

Brave New World
Aldous Huxley

Aldous Huxley's *Brave New World* is one of the great works of science fiction.

It is the year After Ford 632 in the New World. People are born and live by scientific methods. There is worldwide happiness and order. Then John comes from the Savage Reservation to the New World and with him he brings strong emotions – love, hate, anger, fear. Suddenly, danger threatens the New World.

There are hundreds of Penguin Readers to choose from – world classics, film adaptations, modern-day crime and adventure, short stories, biographies, American classics, non-fiction, plays ...

For a complete list of all Penguin Readers titles, please contact your local Pearson Longman office or visit our website.

www.penguinreaders.com

The Chamber
John Grisham

The horror of death row is that you die a little each day. The waiting kills you.

Seventy-year-old Sam Cayhall is on Mississippi's death row. Sam hates lawyers but his date with the gas chamber is close, and time is running out. Then Adam Hall, a young lawyer arrives. Can he and his secret persuade Sam to accept his help?

Man from the South and Other Stories
Roald Dahl

Roald Dahl is the master of the unexpected. Things are not always what they seem and nobody should be trusted. In this collection of his short stories we learn some strange lessons about the dangerous world we live in. But you will have to wait until the final pages of each story to discover the last, terrible twist!

Memoirs of a Geisha
Arthur Golden

Memoirs of a Geisha is one of the great stories of our time.

We follow Sayuri's life: her early years in a small fishing village and as a geisha in Gion. And throughout her struggle, we know of her secret love for the only man who ever showed her any kindness – a man who *seems* to be out of her reach.

There are hundreds of Penguin Readers to choose from – world classics, film adaptations, modern-day crime and adventure, short stories, biographies, American classics, non-fiction, plays ...

For a complete list of all Penguin Readers titles, please contact your local Pearson Longman office or visit our website.

www.penguinreaders.com

Longman Dictionaries

Express yourself with confidence!

*Longman has led the way in ELT dictionaries since 1935.
We constantly talk to students and teachers around the
world to find out what they need from a learner's dictionary.*

Why choose a Longman dictionary?

Easy to understand

Longman invented the Defining Vocabulary – 2000 of the most
common words which are used to write the definitions in our
dictionaries. So Longman definitions are always clear and easy
to understand.

Real, natural English

All Longman dictionaries contain natural examples taken from
real-life that help explain the meaning of a word and show you
how to use it in context.

Avoid common mistakes

Longman dictionaries are written specially for learners, and we
make sure that you get all the help you need to avoid common
mistakes. We analyse typical learners' mistakes and include
notes on how to avoid them.

Innovative CD-ROMs

Longman are leaders in dictionary CD-ROM innovation. Did
you know that a dictionary CD-ROM includes features to help
improve your pronunciation, help you practice for exams and
improve your writing skills?

**For details of all Longman dictionaries, and to choose
the one that's right for you, visit our website:**

www.longman.com/dictionaries